GREENHOUSE GARDENING
FOR
BEGINNERS

The Complete Step-by-Step Guide to Build Your Own Fit-for-Purpose Greenhouse and Grow Organic Vegetables, Fruits, Herbs, and Flowers; All-Year-Round. (Bonus: 10 Greenhouse Plans Included)

MICHAEL YORK

TABLE OF CONTENTS

INTRODUCTION TO GREENHOUSES

Who loves a garden, loves a greenhouse too. —William Cowper

The Origins of Greenhouses

There is no denying that the human race has been experimenting with managed plant cultivation environments since Roman times. Naturally, these ancient people had more primal methods compared to modern-day practices. Be that as it might, it's wonderful to think that garden enthusiasts were already around since that era.

Greenhouse gardening became more widespread in the United Kingdom (UK) and Netherlands during the 17th century. Even though these elaborate and colossal structures were not very practical, the daily close up during the night and winter was also tiresome. However, it does bear mentioning that it served its purpose, even with the cumbersome operational requirements.

It is said that the first modernized version of a greenhouse we've come to know today was invented by Charles Lucien Bonaparte (yes, he was a nephew of Napoleon I). He was a French botanist and built the first pragmatic greenhouse during the 1800s in the Netherlands. At the time, he aimed to cultivate tropical plants and plants with medicinal properties.

The Victorian era in the UK can be categorized as the golden years of greenhouse infrastructure. The English built large greenhouses, and the upper class, in particular, tried to outdo one another in attempting to make a greenhouse more elaborate than the other.

5 Curious Greenhouse Facts

There are many interesting and chatty facts to share about greenhouses. Some of these facts include:

- Some estimate that there are currently more than 9,000,000 acres of greenhouse property worldwide.
- One of the best things about greenhouses is that they can be used all year round and installed in any climatic environment. It makes no difference if you live in an area with predominantly hot or cold weather, you can manipulate your greenhouse to work for you!
- Personal greenhouses range between 50-200 sq ft. And commercial greenhouses can reach up to 100,000 sq ft.
- Did you know that the glass used to construct greenhouses needs to be free from any air bubbles? If not, those bubbles act like a magnifying glass, potentially burning your plants.
- The glass used to make greenhouses should be of horticultural grade.

Greenhouses as a Rewarding Hobby

Once seen as a luxury experience only reserved for the wealthy, more and more 'greenies' are turning to this as a hobby. The upper class had the uncanny ability to force fruits and exotic flowers to grow out of season through to full bloom and harvest. The modern greenhouse is smaller in stature and can be proportionally erected in almost any home environment. The plant collections of today are just as exotic, and it's great to cultivate scarce plants that are often expensive to buy. Today's greenhouse gardeners use their structures for anything from herbaceous plants to tree propagation.

With the sharp increase in energy costs, the modernized greenhouse has become more common than ever. Notably, one of the significant drawbacks is that it doesn't retain heat well, even though solar energy is collected. This is why a backup heating system may be a good investment, although it can be expensive to operate. However, the modern greenhouse hobbyist can utilize a range of tactics such as purchasing insulation blankets, air-inflated covers, and even double-glazing. These methods have since proven to reduce heating costs by at least 50% (Totemeier, 1981).

Top-Rated Greenhouse Gardening Benefits

There are many benefits associated with greenhouse gardening. Some firm favorites to highlight include:

- It's multi-purpose: Versatility is one of the best features of a greenhouse. You can basically grow anything in the structure and even change it up as often as you'd like.

- Your one-stop gardening space: Another great reason to invest in a greenhouse is that you have one dedicated spot on your premises for all things gardening. You don't need a separate shed as you can also store all your garden implements in the structure.

- Constant returns: Not only can you decide how often, and which returns (in terms of harvest) you want, you don't have to be concerned about environmental factors hampering plant growth. In addition, you can now produce happy and healthy plants for 365 days of the year.

- Protection for plants: Not only are plants protected against environmental factors but growing them in a greenhouse means they are protected against various pests as well (more on this in a later chapter).

- Stable temperature control: You can now enjoy an extended growing season employing an optimum environment with a steady temperature. Even if you are new to this hobby, you'll quickly learn that plants thrive in humid, warm environments that enhance growth.

- Design freedom: You can completely customize your greenhouse design so that it suits your surroundings. Your design can be visually appealing, and add value to your garden.

- Cost and energy efficiency: From a financial perspective, greenhouses can be cost-effective by reducing your monthly grocery bill. Also, it's easy to spend a lot of money and never be satisfied with the number of flowers in your garden. You will have more than enough space to grow hundreds, if not thousands of different seedlings at a time. With this comes the option of trading plants amongst friends thereby, never having to buy more plants, seeds, or flowers again.

- They're great for your health: Spending time in nature is just the remedy to rid your physical and mental being from everyday stresses. For example, greenhouses armed with diffused lighting have been proven to alleviate Seasonal Affective Disorder (SAD). You'll never find a more natural mood booster than this (Rogers, 2016).

- Chemical-free foods: Another great benefit worth mentioning is that you know your food is grown without pesticides unlike produce from a retail store, or greengrocer. There's nothing better than wholesome, chemical-free foods.

- Financial returns: You can generate income through a greenhouse gardening business by selling freshly cultivated produce at markets. Another suggestion is to use your harvests to make specialty items such as organic jams and sauces, which you can then sell to supermarkets or restaurants. The possibilities are literally endless!

Before diving in, it's crucial to note that this is the only greenhouse gardening book you'll ever need. The book is divided into two parts:

Part One: How to Plan and Build Your Greenhouse Structure

This portion will cover all the structures and equipment you'll need to start your greenhouse journey. Despite many readers only showing interest in growing plants, getting the fundamentals *just* right is equally important.

Part Two: How to Grow Plants

This section will include a complete step-by-step blueprint on growing:

- Herbs
- Plants
- Flowers
- Fruits
- Tropical plants
- Vegetables

With all this must-have information at your fingertips, you have the required tools and details to start and run your greenhouse successfully.

Without further ado, let's proceed.

PART ONE:
HOW TO PLAN AND BUILD YOUR GREENHOUSE STRUCTURE

CHAPTER 1:
CHOOSING YOUR GREENHOUSE

Greenhouse Zoning and Building Permits

Before deciding which greenhouse you need, it's necessary to complete your due diligence with regard to building and zoning permits. The last thing you need is to fill your shopping basket, ready to get cracking, just to find out your greenhouse doesn't meet the local code requirements.

Every country and individual community is different, so there is no one-size-fits-all answer and solution for the required permits. The good news is that investigating your local requirements is a relatively painless process, which you can do yourself.

Two permits need to be considered when you are buying or building a greenhouse.

Zoning permits

Each newbie greenhouse gardener is responsible for identifying the permit requirements. Zoning permits are in place to regulate the location of the greenhouse on your premises. For instance, a zoning permit will include how close to the lot lines you can build. This is determined by your individual community regulations and rules. Some communities may require that a greenhouse be erected at least 20 feet away from lot lines. But, again, every neighborhood is unique, so ensure that you check this beforehand.

In some instances, zoning permits will govern the number of greenhouses or accessory buildings you can construct on your property. Other accessory items that fall under this category include outbuildings and sheds. Another crucial factor is the size of the planned greenhouse. For instance, your local zoning department may decide that a greenhouse smaller than 200 square feet does not require a building permit.

Lastly, after your zoning permit requirements are met, you might have to get a building permit, as mentioned earlier.

Building permits

Building permits are normally issued by your county, provincial, or regional building department. The relevant building codes are based on the physical appearance and structural integrity of a building.

It's true that in most rural areas, building permits may not be required, however, urban areas will have some regulatory sandboxes (pun intended) pertaining to these. Building codes require that the structural integrity of a greenhouse can withstand environmental elements such as snow and wind loads specific to your geographical location.

Whether you are purchasing an attached or freestanding greenhouse will have an impact on the type of permit. Attached greenhouses typically require a building permit because they are considered an addition to your house and are not viewed as an "accessory building." Instead, attached greenhouses are treated much like adding a sunroom to your home.

In the instance of building codes and building appearance, this will vary greatly in each community. Some may have regulations on the appearance of an accessory building. The reason behind the implementation of such rules is to govern the general aesthetic appearance of a neighborhood. Most communities will welcome the idea of greenhouses with open arms. However, some corporations, condo groups, and homeowners' associations may have stricter requirements. It's entirely possible that each association might have its own review board that needs to approve each design on a case-by-case basis. Should any association decline your request, you can apply for a variance. Variances are possible because communities are encouraged by the idea of organic gardening and will endeavor to accommodate these disputes.

Regardless of your location, any experienced greenhouse designer or manufacturer will generally guide you through the required regulations in your area. Some might even offer support by applying for variances to the relevant association on your behalf.

CHAPTER 2:
GREENHOUSE CLASSIFICATIONS AND TYPES

There are many factors to consider regarding the type of greenhouse suited to your needs. This chapter is dedicated to all the factors you need to consider before starting your journey. First, let's look at three different classifications of greenhouses.

Three Greenhouse Classifications

Greenhouses can be categorized into three primary classes.

Attached Greenhouses

Exactly as the name implies, these greenhouses are physically attached to the gardener's house.

Freestanding or Independent Greenhouses

The most basic version of this structure comprises an oblong-shaped box with a center beam and two sloped roofs. The beam is crafted from one-piece of wood or metal and added to the apex of the sloped roof for support

Gutter-Connected Greenhouses

This is a range of two or more free-standing greenhouse structures joined together at the eave line. A gutter is provided at the common joint eave to collect rain run-off.

Types of Greenhouses

There are several different greenhouses, each with its own intricacies, requirements, pros, and cons. So let's take a deep dive into the various classifications and the details around them.

While contemplating which greenhouse to invest in, it's imperative to note that different types of greenhouses serve different purposes, plants, and circumstances. As a result, the type of greenhouse you pick will largely depend on your requirements. But, exactly how are greenhouses categorized? What makes each one unique, and how do you select the one best suited to your individual requirements?

A-Frame Greenhouses

This is one of the most common types of greenhouses. Due to the simplicity in erecting these structures, they are trendy amongst greenies, as it only requires a single inverted V-structure.

These greenhouses work exceptionally well in south-facing backyards and spaces.

Average Cost per sq ft: Between $5–$25

Ease of Build

This greenhouse is ideal for beginners due to its low cost, quick build, and common design. In addition to this, the structure also heats up quickly.

Main Feature

It is attractive, robust, and stable if rods or stakes are used to anchor the greenhouse. In addition, A-frames can be made stronger and wider than rebar structures.

Main Advantages

- Simplistic design.
- Minimum materials required during construction.

Main Drawbacks

- Proper air circulation is problematic in the corners.
- Sidewalls are too narrow to make full use of the greenhouse.

Chinese Greenhouses

These greenhouses have been designed to use insulation and thermal mass in a bid to retain as much heat as possible. With this in mind, it's an excellent structure for growing crops throughout the year. In rural areas with little energy input available, this structure can operate on solar energy alone. With the population's increase in sustainability awareness, many gardeners in China have built these structures in recent decades.

Average Cost per sq ft: Approximately $1.50

Ease of Build

If you are looking for a low-maintenance option during the summer months, this design might prove challenging to maintain. Growing crops in summer will take some practice and research, and might not be a viable option for a beginner.

However, through patience, perseverance, and using greenhouse gardening communities, the reward will pay off in the long run.

Main Feature

While cost per square foot may seem low, the volume of materials may increase the price tag for this model. But, they yield a range of features that make them great, such as being earth-sheltered and containing thermal mass to regulate heat.

Main Advantages

- Increases land conservation.
- Easy and cheap to construct.
- Reduces soil erosion.

Main Drawbacks

- High humidity can promote plant diseases and pests.

Cold Frame Greenhouses

If you are in the market to extend your growing season, this structure is your solution! Out of all the greenhouses, it's the most straightforward option and the least expensive. It's as simple as using your desired frame structure, covered with a material such as plastic or glass and then placing it over the garden. In addition, it has great plant protection capabilities against environmental elements for something so condensed. This is an excellent solution if you want a greenhouse set up in your garden, even if it's small.

Average Cost per sq ft: Between $0.50–$1.00

Ease of Build

Cold frame greenhouses are relatively easy to construct, making them effortless for beginners and cost-saving purposes.

Main Advantages

- Startup costs are manageable.
- It's effortless to construct the design.
- It can be crafted from recycled materials.

Main Drawbacks

- Cold frame greenhouses tend to overheat.
- Structural and plant risks are involved in using repurposed materials to craft the greenhouse.

Even Span Greenhouses

This greenhouse, also called an American Even Span Greenhouse (high-profile), is easily distinguished by its two sloping roofs. This design can be used to set up a small greenhouse in your yard or garden, and can be adjusted according to measurements. Various options are at your disposal, such as letting it stand on its own, or attaching one end to your house. There's also the possibility of expanding it to accommodate more rows and shelves.

These greenhouses are crafted from materials such as clear glass that aid in adequate sunlight seeping into the plants. One major drawback is the large area the structure can cover which impacts heating costs. You'd have to invest in a heating system to protect your plants during winter.

Examples

The Venlo

One example of this type of structure is the Venlo, or low-profile greenhouse. It's crafted from galvanized steel and supported by a gable glass roof. It was designed to use single glass panes from the top to the gutter. No girts or purlins are used in the roof structure, maximizing light transmission and promoting energy efficiency. The Venlo is ideally suited for produce that needs maximum sunlight.

Type: Attached

Average Cost per sq ft: Approximately $25

Ease of Build

This is a great option for newbie greenies since it can be adapted to small growing spaces and is quite easy to build.

Main Advantages

- Flexible design with no size limitations.
- Ability to hold a large number of plants.
- The shape can maintain temperature uniformity.
- No rain or snow accumulation, thanks to the A-framed roof.

Main Drawbacks

- Expensive start-up costs.
- A separate heating system is required.

Geodesic Greenhouses

Geodesic greenhouses, or Geodomes for short, have many attributes that make them ideal for backyard food gardening. The dome shape creates a large interior, with a minimal surface area, yielding plenty of vertical or window gardening space. The form can also maximize exposure to the sun, meaning your plants will gain sunlight from all angles inside the dome.

One of the greenhouse's standout features is its durability. The triangles that make up the dome do not require internal supports as they can distribute weight evenly.

Average Cost per sq ft: Between $10–$25

Ease of Build

Adding a geodome greenhouse is a great option if you want an aesthetically pleasing feature in your garden. An added bonus is the ease of installation due to various options at your disposal.

Main Advantages

- Holds up well in all climates.
- Size is easily scalable based on requirements.
- Easy to construct as a DIY project.

Main Drawbacks

- Some ready-made geodome kits can compromise on quality of materials, posing risks later.

Gothic Arch Greenhouses

This greenhouse has an intricate goth-like design structure. Its distinctly pointed roof eliminates the need for trusses. It's perfectly suited to the greenies interested in hobby or commercial greenhouse endeavors as it can be as big or small as you'd like.

After carefully pondering the pros and cons associated with this greenhouse, the only thing left for you to do is to consider space and budget limitations.

Type: Round arch greenhouse

Average Cost per sq ft: Between $10–$15

Ease of Build

This might be an ideal option as a greenhouse for a beginner gardener since it can be scaled to size.

Main Advantages

- Boasts size versatility.
- Aesthetically pleasing.
- Rain and snow are easily drained.
- No trusses are required.

Main Drawbacks

- Requires more unique materials compared to other greenhouse types.
- Inability to promote adequate air circulation to the corners.

Hotbed Greenhouses

These greenhouses are essentially heated cold frames. It is similar to a mini greenhouse, as it yields the same benefits at little cost. This design is commonly used to extend the plant growing season and boost the cultivation of warm-season veggies such as peppers and tomatoes.

A southern exposure where the best sunlight is received is ideal for this structure A north or northwest windbreak can be applied to reduce heating costs. This can be achieved using hay or straw bales, or an evergreen hedge.

Average Cost per sq ft: Between $0.00–$1.00

Ease of Build

The hotbed greenhouse can be a great starter structure if you keep it simple and focus on the basics. Other provisions include having the right tools and already having good DIY capabilities or being prepared to watch many YouTube tutorials.

Main Advantages

- The structure can be used all year round.
- Small or large crops can be cultivated.
- Additional winter heating may not be required depending on the plant varieties used.

Main Drawbacks

- Possible high costs upfront.
- Risk of pest infestations.

Lean-to Greenhouses

This greenhouse is typically placed against the side of a building, however, it can be placed between two buildings or against one wall. To be fully enclosed, two to three sides and the roof will require coverage with a greenhouse sheeting material.

Most lean-to greenhouses aren't taller than 12 ft and can only hold one or two rows of plants at any given time. You have the option of extending it against a taller wall but ensure it receives adequate daily sunlight.

Type: Attached, freestanding

Average Cost per sq ft: Between $10–$25

Ease of Build

This can be an excellent starter greenhouse if you are unsure about how committed you plan to be. It's one of the most cost-effective types of greenhouses.

Main Advantages

- Typically located close to water and energy resources.
- Fewer startup costs incurred towards the materials.
- Needs minimal setup space.
- Minimal roof support involved.

Main Drawbacks

- Limited planting space.
- Lack of proper light exposure might hamper optimal plant development.
- Due to the wall sides, temperature control might prove challenging.
- The supporting wall might limit height.

Sawtooth Greenhouses

This greenhouse model uses optimal ventilation and can withstand different loads. The arch shape is optimal for light transmission. The roof structure ventilation can provide 25% of the required operational ventilation with the addition of the side ventilation as well.

The structure is versatile enough in that different technical solutions can be applied to achieve the same goal. This design promotes effective hot air removal from inside the greenhouse. The roof vent is primarily used on hoop houses and is similar to Chinese greenhouses.

Average Cost per sq ft: Approximately $9.00

Ease of Build

This greenhouse boasts a very simplistic design that is fairly easy to erect at home, making it the perfect option for a starter 'greenie'.

Main Advantages

- Ideally suited to small commercial establishments and hobbyists.
- Only one side requires a roll-up.
- Promotes natural air flow within the structure.
- Ability to auto vent the roof without using fans when simplistic technology is applied (the beeswax actuator method).
- Compatible with swamp coolers for tropical climates.
- Start small and expand at any time.
- Construction is medium complexity.
- Inexpensive materials can be used during construction.

Main Drawbacks

- The structure has more shade than sunlight.
- Only a low volume of air is enclosed in the chapel.

Ridge and Furrow Greenhouses

This type of greenhouse has an A-frame structure. The design is achieved by attaching the A-frame shapes in a row. Each row is connected at the eave, providing drainage for excess rain and snow.

Ridge and furrow greenhouses are primarily used on farmlands for large-scale harvest and production, where the greenhouse keeper maintains many greenhouses and seeks protection against environmental elements. The number of greenhouses is connected, thus creating a bigger growing region, increasing site protection against harsh sunlight from penetrating. This greenhouse type is cost and energy-efficient and aids the greenhouse gardener in caring for the plants between the greenhouses.

Example

One example of this design is the mini walk-in greenhouse. It's very versatile as it can be used indoors or outdoors. The A-frame structure is clearly distinguishable and can be set up in the ridge and furrow method. The setup is straightforward, as you only need to place the greenhouse sides to each other and open the ends to make one large space.

This is an excellent option as manufacturers deploy high-quality aluminum to construct the product. This implies that the product is durable and corrosion-resistant. Another great feature is the A-frame roof structure ensures ample heat distribution to all the

plants inside. Lastly, this greenhouse has eight plant shelves and requires less than five hours to erect if the instructions are followed.

Type: Freestanding, gutter-connected

Average Cost per sq ft: Between $35–$40

Ease of Build

This is an excellent option to consider for beginner greenhouse gardeners.

Main Advantages

- Ample space for plant structure.
- Energy and automation are efficient.
- Adequate drainage capabilities.
- Visually appealing.

Main Drawbacks

- Expensive start-up costs.
- Significant space requirements.

Quonset Greenhouses

These greenhouses are sometimes called polyethylene tunnels (this term is discussed in a later chapter) or hoop houses. They can be crafted from materials such as metal, plastic and PVC. During construction, the materials are bent into hoop-like shapes and covered with polyethylene film.

Ventilation takes place through large open doors and roll-up sidewalls. These hoop houses are fitted with end walls that can be opened to promote ventilation. One drawback of a hoop house is that it lacks permanent environmental control mechanisms and foundations. Notably, in some US states, the permits and regulations are less intense than for other greenhouse structures.

Average Cost per sq ft: Between $10–$15

<u>Ease of Build</u>

This is one of the best greenhouses for beginner greenies since the structure is as easy to erect as it is to break down, making it an ideal option if you wish to move the structure to a different location later.

<u>Main Advantages</u>

- Free-standing architecture promotes the greatest amount of sunlight.
- Best suited to growing plants from seedlings.
- Simple to erect.

<u>Main Drawbacks</u>

- Expensive to construct from scratch.
- More support structures are required due to the uneven design.

Uneven Span Greenhouses

This type of greenhouse can be easily recognized as it's quite literally exactly what it says. The name is derived from the fact that one roof of the structure is shorter than the other. The design's main purpose is to promote more sunlight intake when the structure is located in a steep-sloped or high-hill area.

Ideally, the longer side of the greenhouse needs to be transparent and face the south side. Due to most greenhouses now located in flat, even areas, this type of greenhouse is no longer prevalent and scarcely observed.

Average Cost per sq ft: Between $10–$15

<u>Ease of Build</u>

This can be a great homemade greenhouse option if you have the space.

<u>Main Advantages</u>

- Aids in sunlight reaching the plants.
- Wind-resistant.
- Long-lasting and robust construction.

<u>Main Drawbacks</u>

- Not suited to flat areas.

Walipini Greenhouses

This is an underground greenhouse with a clear or translucent roof. The name *walipini* is derived from an indigenous Bolivian tribe that spoke the Aymara language. These greenhouses are unique because they use the earth to establish an environment with a stable temperature. This yields a higher produce turnover where you can cultivate many different plants with little energy resources. In short, it provides the ideal warm climate for optimal plant growth.

Average Cost per sq ft: $10–$15

Ease of Build

Creating a pit with this minimalist design is easy. This structure is beginner approved.

Main Advantages

- Uses of passive energy.
- No mechanical intervention required.
- Warmer underground than above the ground in winter.

Main Drawbacks

- Expensive to construct.
- Labor intensive.
- Durability concerns.

Window-Mounted Greenhouses

These structures are usually connected to a south window of a house. These greenhouses are ideal for beginner gardeners to indulge in their favorite hobby all year round. You can grow anything from herbs to decorative plants right in the comfort of your home.

Type: Attached

Average Cost per sq ft: Approximately $2.50

Ease of Build

Window-mounted greenhouses are a great DIY project and very straightforward to construct.

Main Advantages

- Inexpensive to install.
- Can be used inside your home.
- Warming your house utilizing passive solar heat.

Main Drawbacks

- Space constraints limit the number of plants that can be cultivated at any given time.

Expansion and Modular Greenhouses

Expansion greenhouses make reconfiguration easy at any time. Expansion is effortless through a series of pre-established components . You can go as big as your available space. This is a great option for urban greenhouse farmers. There are a range of advantages when it comes to modular greenhouses.

You can consider buying greenhouses composed of multiple modules. You should plan the required space in advance in case you want to install additional modules in the future.

CHAPTER 3:
GREENHOUSE SIZING

Before erecting a greenhouse, one must consider how best to use the space inside. Sadly, many greenhouse gardeners don't think ahead when sizing their greenhouse and how they plan to use the area. This can result in frustration and an overall unsavory experience.

Luckily, greenhouse gardeners can invest in the correct size greenhouse for their desires and needs with a little forethought. However, it's crucial to examine the available widths of greenhouses and how this will affect the structure's overall layout for optimum space utilization.

Greenhouse Widths

Greenhouses come in an array of widths and lengths. When considering the floor plan or your greenhouse layout, you should be more concerned with the width than the length. This is because, in most cases, the width will determine the parameters and dimensions of aisles and benches.

Benches are used by most greenhouse hobbyists. You can determine the bench type and aisle spacing when focussing on width during your planning stage.

Hobby greenhouses are typically between eight to ten feet wide, but some can also range between 12–20 feet in width. Industrial, production or commercial greenhouses are typically wide, spanning 20 feet or more.

Let's explore the different typical greenhouse widths.

8 Feet

Many hobby greenhouses span eight feet wide, but it does not represent the structure's outside dimensions, which means that this measurement does not consider the frame. This implies that the actual width of the inside walls will be less than eight feet.

Hobby greenhouses of eight feet generally have benches two feet wide on both sides of a three-foot wide aisle. Although this might sound ideal for some greenie horticulturists, many hobbyists will quickly fill up the bench space and want more.

10 Feet

This is another popular size option for beginner gardeners, as it instantly provides 30% more bench space than the eight-foot option mentioned previously. The typical dimensions of a ten-footer are having three-foot benches on either side of a three-foot wide aisle setup. A three-foot bench is ideal as it provides adequate space without being too deep, making it hard to reach the crops. Overall, the ten-foot option is a great starter size and comfortable to manage.

12-20 Feet

Greenhouses that fall under this size range are the perfect choice for plants in more places than just the benches. For example, greenies can implement raised beds or cultivate sets of tropical plants that require extra headspace.

This is another good option for beginner hobbyists. It allows you to include features such as a seating bench, a water feature, or any other decorative additions to your garden area. Remember that these additions will take up space, so they must be planned carefully.

Greater Than 20 Feet

Widths greater than 20 feet are reserved for industrial, commercial, or educational applications. These structures typically have two three-foot aisles, with three-foot benches on either side and a footstool in the center, generally between six and eight feet in width. This is an excellent option if you are looking to optimize gardening space.

What Determines the Size of a Greenhouse?

In most cases, the intended application and available space will be the key determining factors of your greenhouse size. Most noteworthy greenhouse manufacturers will assist you in choosing the best size suited to your needs and available space. Some will even go as far as to help with the planning and space optimization inside the greenhouse.

Industrial vs. Private Greenhouses

Now, depending on how far you are prepared to go with your hobby, there are two other key differences that you'd need to consider.

Industrial Greenhouses

A commercial or industrial greenhouse is a structure that produces crops sold for commercial consumption. These are high-tech greenhouses designed to grow the predetermined crops for sale. Many greenhouses boast see-through roofs that allow sunlight to stream through. Others use special lights to replicate the sunlight.

Industrial greenhouses exposed to natural sunlight or artificial alternatives are warmer inside than the external temperature, which acts as a barrier against cold weather. The warm air cannot escape, thus the temperature rises inside the structure.

Commercial greenhouses typically have a financial stake in crop yields, and are crucial to the operation's profitability. Artificial coolers and heaters are used to control the greenhouse's temperature, and ventilation. This implies that the temperature controls will play a pivotal part in deciding whether the greenhouse will be used commercially or restricted to private use.

How Do Commercial Greenhouses Work?

It makes no difference if the greenhouse is for private or industrial use, its premise stays the same. Simply put, the structure enables the sunlight to warm the space and encourage the plants to grow. When the greenhouse's microclimate can be controlled, it can extend the growing season by a few weeks or even months.

One significant difference is that industrial growers will engage a scientific approach to each process step to ensure optimum crop yields. A commercial greenhouse owner will deploy any and all best-growth practices in their arsenal.

Private Greenhouses

A non-commercial or private greenhouse has sides and a roof constructed mainly from glass or other transparent materials, where the humidity and temperature can be controlled. Home greenhouse gardeners will use greenhouses for cultivatingout-of-season plants and food for personal consumption. We will focus on the latter type of greenhouse in this book.

Low/Medium and High Technology Greenhouses

Greenhouses are seen as a technology-based investment. The health and productivity of your crop yields are tightly governed by controlling the conditions in which the plants are grown. For investment purposes, we will discuss the three categories used to assist a new gardener in selecting the best greenhouse for their requirements and budget.

Low-Tech

A large proportion of the greenhouse industry in Australia, for example, makes use of lowtech structures and buildings which are less than three meters in height. The most common form of a low-technology greenhouse is the tunnel house or igloo kind.

A negative associated with this structure is the lack of vertical walls, resulting in issues with poor ventilation. Little to no automation is used, and they're inexpensive and effortless to construct.

While this design provides benefits over field productions, the growing conditions potentially limit yields, and the crops are not easy to manage. Low-level tech structures create a suboptimal growing condition, limiting yield production and providing no barrier against diseases and pests. As a result, chemicals must be introduced to keep infestations at bay.

Although low-tech greenhouses have environmental limitations and significant production restrictions, they are a great stepping stone into the industry with their cost-saving features.

Medium-Tech

Medium-tech buildings are typically categorized by vertical walls higher than two meters but less than four, and have an apex of less than five and a half meters. They can have sidewalls, roof ventilation, or a combination of both. These greenhouses use varying levels of automation and are typically clad single or double style with glass or plastic film.

Medium-level greenhouses are the best midrange solution between productivity and cost, representing an environmental and economic basis for the greenhouse industry.

The production in these types of greenhouse structures can prove to be more efficient than in the fields, as the implementation of hydroponic systems can proliferate the efficient use of water resources.

The full potential of greenhouse horticulture is hard to attain, but many non-chemical products and pest management strategies are at your disposal.

High-Tech

High-technology greenhouses boast a wall at least four meters high with an apex of eight meters above the ground (Department of Primary Industries, n.d.). These greenhouse structures have high environmental performance and superior crop yields.

Greenhouse structures of this kind can have sidewall ventilation, roof ventilation, or both. The greenhouse is covered in double or single thickness glass or polycarbonate sheeting.

The environmental controls are primarily automated and promote environmental and economic sustainability in this structure. With all these amazing features, it is no surprise that these greenhouses don't use many pesticides.

Not only are these structures a sight to behold, but they are being used more often by agribusiness enthusiasts.

CHAPTER 4:
PLANNING FOR YOUR GREENHOUSE

Budgeting for a Greenhouse

The most frequently asked question about erecting a new greenhouse is whether buying or building is cheaper. Buying a greenhouse kit can be cost-prohibitive for people, especially considering a larger structure or one with built-in automation that can control temperature, light, etc.

Quality produced ready-made greenhouses typically start at a few hundred dollars and can reach tens of thousands, if not more. Therefore, it makes sense to inquire about the setup and costs of a Do It Yourself (DIY) greenhouse structure to save on start-up costs. This will also prevent beginner greenhouse keepers from forking out large sums of money but still optimizing the space and getting the design they truly want.

Sure, factors like materials will determine cost, but building a structure from preloved materials or cheaper ones is highly possible. Yard sales, auctions, and online trading groups on platforms such as Facebook can be a great place to start.

Greenhouse Cost Factors

Whether you want to start a whole new project or are looking for ways to diversify an existing greenhouse structure, there are some external cost voices that will determine if you are unrestricted or limited in your choice of greenhouse. Some of these include location, space, and climate, which will impact your investment's spend.

The most crucial decision you will make is the types of produce you'd want to grow. This selection and the external limitations mentioned will give you a good idea of what will be needed inside to grow your plants and the associated costs.

All of the resources needed inside your greenhouse are called internal factors and can include the following:

- automation
- climate control
- fertigation
- forced or natural ventilation
- irrigation
- labor

All of these aforementioned factors combined will impact the required investment to get your greenhouse in working order and, in turn, influence productivity in the future.

In the case of commercial greenhouse costs, long-term thinking will be required. Even though the initial capital will seem overwhelming, one must look ahead at the benefits of increased crop yields.

If your available capital is limited, it's essential to take it back to the basics by developing your greenhouse with expansion in mind, such as in the case of modular greenhouses. If expanding is a forethought, you need to invest in a system that's flexible and scalable enough to produce higher yields.

These factors will also directly influence the type of greenhouses for your unique situation and needs.

CHAPTER 5:
OTHER DECIDING GREENHOUSE FACTORS

Now that you've got a pretty good idea of the types and typical costs associated with greenhouse structures, there are a few other considerations, which include:

- airflow
- CO2 generators
- dimensions
- flooring
- foundations
- frame
- glazing
- humidity
- irrigation systems
- location
- temperature control
- wind securing

Airflow

It is said that Horizontal Airflow (HAF) is the best option for greenhouse circulation. Before the existence of HAF systems, finding a 10°F to 15°F difference in temperature at night on opposite sides of the structure was prevalent. This directly impacted the quality and growth of crops. However, with the advancement of HAF systems, you can expect no more than a 2°F difference throughout the greenhouse.

The Basics of HAF

HAF systems operate on the premise that air moves in a consistent horizontal pattern throughout the structure. A greenhouse only requires sufficient energy to tame friction loss and turbulence-meaning the horizontal air only needs to move along.

While it sounds contradictory, air is actually a heavy element. The air per square foot of floor area weighs approximately one pound. Typically, a 30' x 100' greenhouse structure will contain between one and one and a half tons of air. Once the air moves inside, it performs like a car in cruise mode on a level stretch of smooth tar road. This is one of the things that make HAF so efficient. In the greenhouse, you will only require four small-sized fans to keep the air flowing between 50 to 100 feet per minute.

Apart from the uniform temperature feature inside the greenhouse, HAF systems minimize the occurrence of foliar pests and diseases. The moving air eliminates the moisture formed on the plant canopy, making for a drier microclimate. When the temperature of the leaves is permitted to cool much below the air's temperature, it reaches dew point, resulting in condensation that promotes the growth ofdisease-bearing organisms. When one uses radiant cooling on clear nights, especially in greenhouses covered with non-infrared poly material, the crops cool up to seven degrees below air temperature. The good news is that implementing a HAF system can lower the difference.

During the day, the process of photosynthesis consumes the carbon dioxide present in the boundary air layer next to the leaf. Moving air then replaces the depleted air with fresh air containing a high carbon dioxide concentration. A smaller level of elevated carbon dioxide is ordinarily sufficient to yield the same results. For example, the range will be between 800–1000 ppm instead of 1200–1500 ppm.

Common airflow installation mistakes include lower fan capacity, poor fan maintenance, and incorrect fan spacing. Many existing or new systems can be revolutionized with just a little effort. Let's take a look at how these issues can be mitigated.

Providing proper fan capacity

A combined fan capacity of twice the floor area is recommended, to create an efficient system. For instance, a 30' x 100' greenhouse will need a total fan capacity of 6000 cfm. Remember that tall crops such as tomatoes or produce in hanging baskets will require a slightly higher fan capacity to mitigate the additional air turbulence.

Lowering operating costs with low horsepower fans

Small horsepower fans (between 1/10–1/15) can perfectly create the required air movement. In addition, these fans have been designed to move air with less resistance compared to exhaust fans that have been made to overcome air resistance from vents or louvers.

With a permanent split capacitor, you can save as much as one-third on energy costs compared to a shaded pole motor. In addition, if you are planning on using a hot air heating system, they can be compatible with heaters and can be used to replace one small fan, providing the placement is correct. Although this can save on installation costs, it's imperative to note that a heater's fan motor is ½ hp or ⅓, meaning operating costs will be considerably higher.

HAF fans come in blade sizes of 12", 16", 18" and 20" diameters. The fan's output and efficiency will increase the higher the blade diameter. Keep in mind that blade guard design will also play a role in efficacy.

Referring to the earlier example of 6000 cfm, if this were divided by 1675 cfm per fan, the result would be 3.6, meaning that four fans of this size would be adequate.

Correct fan location

The recommendation is to place the first fan between 10' to 15' from the one end wall to piggyback on the air coming around the corner from the opposite side. The other three fans should be placed between 40' to 50' apart to keep the air mass moving. Placing the fans too far apart will result in the air mass short-circuiting to the adjacent air stream and result in a dead air cold spot.

In the instance of a freestanding greenhouse, air moves down one side and back up the opposite side. This creates the circular motion of horizontal air. However, with gutter-connected greenhouses, airflow is more efficient when moved down one bay and back up an adjoining bay. The efficiency then removes the friction between the two contrasting air masses movements.

It's essential to place the fans close to the center of the air mass they are adding energy to. In greenhouse structures with bench or floor crops, it's recommended to place the fans between 7' or 8' above the floor. Today, many greenhouses feature a collar tie or a truss that can aid with support. If you have a greenhouse with hanging baskets, I'd recommend placing the fans just above or just below the basket level to provide energy with the least resistance. Following the recommendations above will also prevent the foliage from drying out in a direct air stream. The ideal placement for fans is below the energy curtain to provide air movement at night and, subsequently, uniform air temperature.

When using a HAF system, it should run for 24 hours a day, except for exhaust fan systems or when the vents (if applicable) are open. This process can be automated by means of implementing a relay switch to the circuit that switches the fans off as soon as the ventilation system is activated. Typical operation costs for one fan are approximately $0.25 at $0.10/kWh of electricity.

Regular maintenance

Maintenance is a crucial role player in accomplishing high efficiency rates. Implementing these pointers below as part of a regular maintenance check will go a long way.

- Remember that fans will regularly be moved out of their original position and should be restrained by a chain or brackets to stop them from moving. When placing the fans, point them directly towards the opposite end wall to convey the maximum number of energy to the resulting air mass.
- Motor casings and fan blade guards gather significant dust from the passing air and must be wiped frequently.
- Air mass movement can be noted by igniting an incense stick behind one of your fans. Before doing so, ensure that the fans run for a few minutes to create the horizontal pattern. Then, carefully observe the resulting smoke to ensure no air short-circuiting occurs. Make use of this opportunity to calculate the airflow rate too.

The advantages of HAF systems have been around for some years. Tweaking your system will significantly increase its efficiency and improve overall performance.

Vertical Airflow

We've already discussed the importance of adequate greenhouse airflow. Vertical Airflow fans (VAF) create an air current forced outward and downward along the walls and roof of greenhouses. The air is then pulled upwards through the plant. As a result, VAF systems produce a uniform environment and reduce energy costs. These fans allow greenies to decrease humidity in an optimized way that's also energy efficient. In addition, they are effortless to mount in greenhouses and even easier to maintain.

Global interest in vertical fans has grown considerably in the last few years. VAF fans can vertically homogenize the air and remove temperature stratification from above to below. These fans also produce level movements by removing microclimates close to plants and aiding the transpiration process.

The biggest drawback of VAF fans is similar to using speed-based fans. VAF systems can't homogenize the environment of the whole area's climate and plants located close to the fans. There is also the issue with crop inconsistency in terms of air distribution. This is a result of buffers or conflict patterns between fans.

The main difference between HAF and VAF systems is that HAF fans move humidity freely and uniformly across the whole greenhouse and promote transpiration.

But what are the types of greenhouse fans at my disposal to choose from?

Types of Greenhouse Fans

Ceiling fans

These fans are designed to handle maximum floor capacity in greenhouse structures with high moisture content. Installing a high-performance, heavy-duty nursery ceiling fan is ideal for summer cooling, winter heating, and removing condensation.

Greenhouse ceiling fans can provide maximum airflow over vast floor areas, improve worker comfort and promote productivity.

Circulation fans

We've focused so much on the crops that I think it's time to also invest in a fan that keeps you cool while you are working. Circulation fans advance a stable climate in greenhouse structures, commercial warehouses, cold frames, and high tunnel systems.

Some advantages of greenhouse circulation fans are reducing heat stress, increasing production levels, and eliminating condensation on roofs and walls. With this fan, you can keep your structure fresher and your workers comfortable.

Duct fans

Tweak your greenhouse ventilation system by installing a duct fan. These fans provide adequate circulation and airflow. There's a range of duct fan accessories available to keep your air supply system working at optimum level, including investing in grilles or dampers.

Most modern duct fans are powerful and quiet—meaning you can zone out and work in your groove while tending to your crops.

Exhaust fans

Eliminate stagnant air in your structure to promote a more productive and healthier plant-growing environment. These fans are versatile in that they reduce worker and crop stress. In addition, exhaust fans are excellent in providing ventilation to cold frames and high tunnel greenhouses. Install this fan type in your greenhouse and create a comfortable and cool growing climate that can improve profitability, productivity, and quality.

Portable fans

Portable greenhouse fans are perfect for cold frames and other greenhouse structures. With a portable fan, you can place circulation and air cooling where needed. The best feature of these fans is that they can easily be located from one point to the next to improve plant quality and worker comfort.

Shrouded and Basket fans

Basket fans throw air in a wider pattern, which negatively impacts the produce below as it yields different air directions, speeds and reduces air uniformity. In turn, this reduces momentum forward as the air from one fan in a series will result in air conflict from a secondary fan because the direction is essentially non-linear. As a result, the second fan will produce an uneven air flow and will have to work harder to push air forward.

Some fan manufacturers such as *Dramm* have developed a formula combining the series layout and the use of shrouded fans. A shrouded fan yields the same force as a basket fan, although via a more direct air blast. *Dramm*'s invention moves the air linearly in one direction down the bay, making a larger width while traveling. When the air is pushed forward, it will train the surrounding air to follow suit when the air is pushed forward.

Shrouded fans work together in a group to push the air forward, creating uniform airflow and decreasing energy use. The use of shrouded fans allows for air intake and produces an exhaust, which are qualities that an unshrouded fan doesn't have. Air intake keeps the momentum going forward by pulling air in the intended direction. These fans are excellent at covering larger distances, lowering the speed needed for momentum-based systems. This implies a greenhouse application that boasts these systems use less energy and require fewer fans.

Speed-Based Airflow vs. Momentum-Based Airflow

A few years ago, HAF systems were only considered for their velocity. But, when the air inside a greenhouse application is moved around, it can be hard to measure velocity

accurately. Conversely, erratic speed bursts can result in temperature instability and an environment that can adversely impact crop growth.

Many people are under the impression that plants have to move for the airflow to do their task efficiently. Notably, while this aids in eliminating microclimate, turbulent air that moves around at high speed is not stable. This implies that some plants will get more air movement than others, resulting in inconsistent transpiration.

For this reason, momentum is busy replacing velocity as the key factor when developing greenhouse airflow mechanisms. Airflow system manufacturers are now aiming to create a uniform air mass that gains momentum as it moves through the structure.

Air momentum might take some time to build up, but doesn't cease to move for a while. If one can move a whole air column in an even motion, the fan systems will be able to wholly reach the inside of a greenhouse. When this process is successful, localized vapor pressure can be removed.

Parallel vs. Series Fan Layouts

Generally, greenies adopt one of two fan position approaches:

Parallel

This is where all the fans are placed on one side of the structure. The air travels through the greenhouse, circulating from the upper air to the lower air, thus making a loop.

Series

This approach is applied when fans are placed in a pattern and move from one end of a structure and move in toward one another.

One issue with the parallel structure is that the system is formulated on the greenhouses being the same size on even ground. Therefore, the parallel setup is not ideal for an uneven piece of land. Furthermore, hills and slopes imply that heat gathers at the apex and the lowest point in the structure remains cool.

Doors, Windows, and Automatic Vents

The chances are high that a greenhouse can overheat, so many greenhouses feature windows to dispel hot air when required. Windows are critical in proper greenhouse ventilation and protecting crops from fungal pests and diseases.I highly recommend that your greenhouse has a good balance of vents and windows and that these equate to one–third of your roof circumference at the very least. Of course, it's not a prerequisite for windows and vents to be positioned right at the roof, but I would advise installing vents at various levels.

Poor ventilation and plant overcrowding can proliferate rapidly, resulting in fungal issues like botrytis, and ultimately, plant death. Summer airflow can be improved by opening the doors and windows to your greenhouse if this does not pose security risks such as tool theft and pilferage by animals seeking food.

Door and window screens can be installed to mitigate most issues, but this can preclude insects from pollinating. Your fruits and veggies need these pollinators. If you still opt to go this route, don't let any outside or inside curtains, blinds, or screens short-circuit the airflow, and regularly inspect the structure for trapped animals and debris to ensure they function properly.

Automatic air vents are an ingenious invention and can be your lifesaver when you cannot tend to your greenhouse daily. Most of these vents are fitted to the roof and open when they sense the temperature outside is rising. The most cost-effective solution is to implement a wax cylinder cycle. When the wax expands, it forces the window open, allowing cool fresh air to enter during the day. At nighttime, the wax contracts again, closing the windows and protecting them against inclimate temperatures outside. These automatic air vents have a lifespan of several years, and replacement parts are commonly available.

_CO_2 Generators_

Before we can delve into the addition of CO_2 generators and how they impact plant growth and other greenhouse factors, we first need to unpack the concept of CO_2 itself.

What is CO_2?

When it comes to plants, the process of photosynthesis involves a chemical reaction between carbon dioxide (CO_2) and water. When exposed to light, it creates sugar (food) for plants and releases oxygen in the atmosphere as a by-product.

Currently, CO_2 makes up 0.04% of our atmospheric volume. That's about 400 parts/million. Carbon dioxide is an odorless and colorless minor gas, but has a life-sustaining task.

Plants consume carbon dioxide during the day via a series of stomata (minute cellular pores) located in the leaves. Next, plant respiration takes place. This is when oxidizedsugar in the plants creates CO_2 and energy. During the process of respiration, plants consume oxygen (O_2) and expel CO_2. This complements the photosynthetic process.

Remember that the carbon dioxide created during the respiration process will always be less than the number of CO_2 consumed during photosynthesis. This means crops are always in a carbon dioxide deficient state, adversely impacting their growth.

The CO² in Plants

Photosynthesis uses CO_2 in the creation of sugar which reduces during the respiration process and promotes plant growth. Environmental and atmospheric elements such as nutrition, water, and humidity affect the pace at which CO_2 is used. As a result, the atmospheric CO_2 will significantly influence crop growth. The carbon dioxide level will be dependent on factors such as:

- combustion
- composting
- number of carbon dioxide sources (water bodies and plants) nearby
- number of carbon dioxide producing industries
- season
- time of day

The naturally occurring level of carbon dioxide can be found in a greenhouse structure featuring adequate ventilation. However, remember that the carbon dioxide concentration inside will be higher than the ambient level outside at night. During the day, the concentration will be lower inside than outside the greenhouse. The level of CO_2 is higher at night because of microbial activities and plant respiration. The CO_2 level could drop to 150 to 200 parts per million inside the greenhouse during the day. This is because plants require CO_2 in the daytime.

When plants are exposed to reduced levels of carbon dioxide, even just for a short while, this can reduce the photosynthetic rate and thus hamper crop growth. When the ambient carbon dioxide level doubles, it will significantly affect product yield. Remember that crops and plants with a C^3 photosynthetic pathway, for example, aster lilies and geraniums, feature a three-carbon element as their first product. This means they respond more to higher carbon dioxide concentrations than plants with a C^4 pathway. You can increase C^3 plant yield by increasing the ambient carbon dioxide concentration to 800-100 ppm.

CO² Greenhouse Supplementation – Pros and Cons

CO_2 supplementation refers to the process of providing additional carbon dioxide to the greenhouse, promoting photosynthesis in crops. Interestingly enough, the advantages of elevated CO_2 levels have been around since the inception of the 19th century and, with it, the need for supplemental carbon dioxide.

Today's greenhouses have a range of advanced automation and related technology. We've developed advancements such as balanced nutrients, improved lighting systems, and we even have control over environmental factors. Thus the only factor that is still limiting is increased CO_2 levels. A greenie only needs to keep these conditions intact by adding CO_2 supplementation to create the ideal environment. Carbon dioxide supplementation is also called carbon dioxide enrichment or carbon dioxide fertilization. Let's look at some of the pros and cons of CO_2 supplementation.

Pros

- Improved biomass production and growth rates as a result of increased photosynthesis.
- More annual crop yields and earlier plant maturity. Due to the time decrease for produce to grow and develop, greenhouse keepers save on fertilization and energy costs.

- When it comes to flowers, adding carbon dioxide yields larger–sized flowers and larger quantities thereof, meaning there's great ROI because of improved product quality.

- Heating costs in winter can be dramatically reduced via supplemental carbon dioxide since this provides extra heat.

- It improves water efficiency and decreases transpiration, which means less water is used during plant production.

Cons

- With a carbon dioxide generation system comes an increase in production costs.

- With the addition of supplemental CO_2, not all plants may respond positively. Therefore you'd need to ensure all the systems are operating together at an optimum level.

- It's been proven that supplemental CO_2 favors younger crops and plants.

- By adding additional CO_2, a greenie would have to check their systems to ensure that the combustion cycle is complete. Gasses such as nitrous oxide, ethylene, and carbon monoxide can result in plant necrosis, senescence, and malformed flowers.

- A greenhouse keeper might have to invest more capital in their greenhouse to add supplemental CO_2 since it's only effective in sealed greenhouses.

- There's also a risk of adding too much carbon dioxide, which can harm humans and plants.

- Maintaining a proper carbon dioxide level in summer is tricky because ventilation is needed to keep the greenhouse cool.

With all these cons, how do we know when it's time to add supplemental CO_2?

When to add supplemental CO_2

As we've just discussed, concentration, timing, and duration determine how effective carbon dioxide supplementation will be. Remember, if all the other greenhouse growing elements operate at optimum level and the greenie is satisfied with crop yields and plant growth, it might not be necessary to add more CO_2. But supplemental carbon dioxide will be advantageous if plants don't reach their full growth potential (generally in fall and spring).

During fall and early spring, your greenhouse vents and windows will be closed most of the time, meaning carbon dioxide availability is limited. Therefore, providing additional carbon dioxide between one to two hours after the sun has come up and ceasing the process between two to three hours before the sun sets again is the perfect time duration for extra carbon dioxide introduction. This is because the photosynthesis process is most active during the exact times mentioned above.

One exception to this rule is vegetables and leafy greens cultivated in a hydroponic system. These applications can be supplemented with carbon dioxide and a grow-lighting system all day and night. When carbon dioxide supplementation is applied to seedlings in flats, crops will be ready for transplant up to two weeks earlier.

The Impact of Supplemental CO² on Plant Growth

Together with other optimal growing conditions, adding supplemental carbon dioxide can play an integral role in improved plant growth and crop yields. Let's take a look at how they work together.

CO² and Light

The photosynthetic rate can't be increased more when the light saturation point has been reached. This implies the maximum light that a plant can use and absorb. However, supplemental carbon dioxide increases the light intensity needed to reach the light saturation point and increases the rate of photosynthesis. During the winter months, the process of photosynthesis is lower due to low light intensity. Adding an extra lighting system will promote the efficiency of carbon dioxide, accelerating the photosynthetic rate and boosting plant growth in the process. An additional lighting system will enhance the efficiency of CO2 and increase the rate of photosynthesis and plant growth.

CO² and Water

The addition of extra carbon dioxide affects plant physiology by regulating the stomata. Increased levels of carbon dioxide semi-close the stomata and decrease conductance. The conductance in the stomata refers to the rate at which carbon dioxide enters and exits water vapor from a leaf's stomata cell. As a result of lower conductance in the stomata, transpiration is minor, and water use is more efficient. These factors then work together to assist plants in coping in water-stressed climates. Therefore we can say that adding carbon dioxide decreases water demand and conserves it when necessary.

CO² and Temperature

The rate of plant growth is widely influenced by creating the optimal temperature. This is because most of a plant's biological growth processes (including photosynthetic rate) increase by implementing a higher temperature. Notably, reaching the best photosynthesis rate depends on the availability of carbon dioxide in the processes. So the higher the availability of carbon dioxide, the higher the plants would want the optimum temperature. Therefore, adding more carbon dioxide increases crop production at higher temperatures, not found in ambient carbon dioxide levels.

CO² and Nutrients

We've already determined that adding carbon dioxide results in rapid plant growth. This is because this newly intensified plant root system can absorb more soil nutrients. One important aspect to remember is that the fertilizer rate also needs to be increased with carbon dioxide supplementation. The reason is that with a standard fertilizer rate, plants can show nutrient deficiency signs because the resource will be exhausted quicker with the introduction of additional carbon dioxide. There aren't any strict recommendations currently available, but this is a good rule of thumb. Bear in mind that certain micronutrients will deplete more rapidly than certain macronutrients. For example, some recent studies have concluded that decreased levels of iron and zinc were found in plants exposed to carbon dioxide supplementation.

Also, lower levels of conductance and transpiration in carbon dioxide supplementations will affect a plant's boron and calcium uptake, which is when additional nutrients must be added to the soil.

CO² Generators in Greenhouses

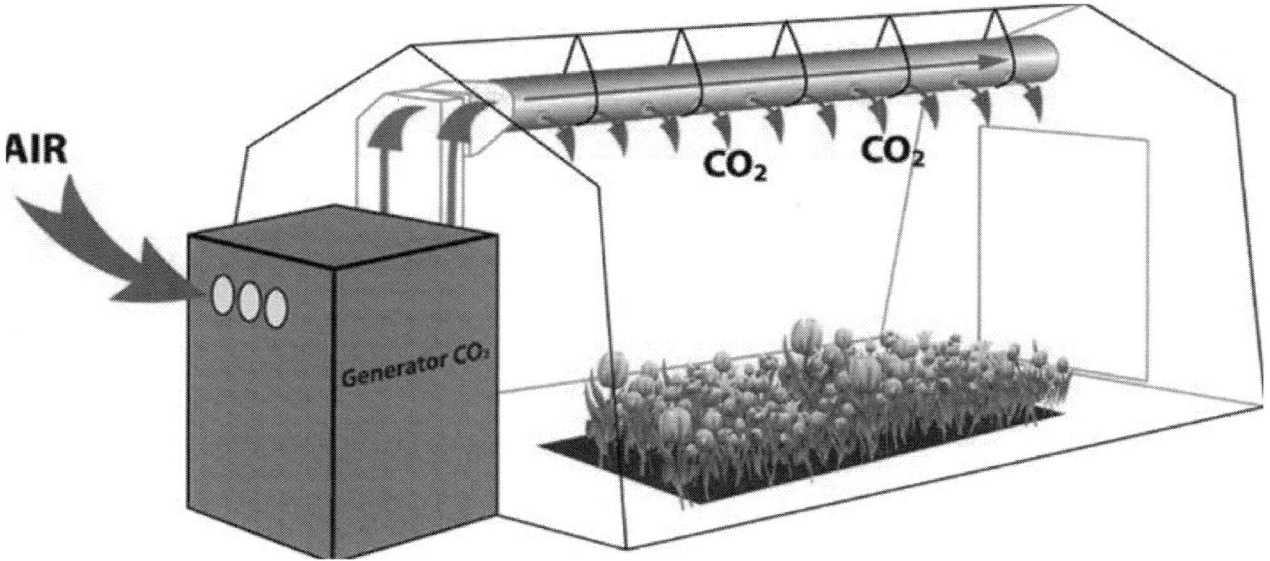

Hydrocarbon fuels that combust create carbon dioxide, heat, and water. Greenhouse owners can install small carbon dioxide generators that operate on natural or propane gas. By burning one pound of gas, a yield of three pounds of carbon dioxide can be expected. One pound of carbon dioxide equals roughly 8.7 cubic feet of gas at standard pressure and temperature. Using this calculation implies that approximately five ounces of ethyl alcohol are needed to control 1300 parts per million carbon dioxide for a greenhouse of 200 sq ft.

The amount of carbon dioxide yields will largely depend on the purity and the type of fuel used. It's equally important to remember that combustion without the required oxygen levels may produce harmful factors to crops due to the impurities released. This can be mitigated by opening smaller areas to introduce fresh air from outside, even if the structure is sealed.

Carbon dioxide generators are installed just above the crops, and each unit can maintain an area of roughly 4,800 sq ft. These units typically cost between $1,000–$2,500 and need an additional $1,00 in gas costs and installation. This carbon dioxide burner ranges between 20,000–60,000 BTU per hour and yields roughly 8.2 pounds of carbon dioxide per hour.

CHAPTER 6:
GREENHOUSE SIZES

Greenhouses primarily come in a vast range of lengths and widths, all in two-foot increments. Settling on a structure type at least six to eight feet wide, will permit you to install shelves on both sides. In addition to the aforementioned, the eaves should be at least five feet tall to allow sufficient light to seep through. You'd find that most newbie greenhouse gardeners wish they had a larger footprint, so to mitigate this, pick the largest one according to your budget and available space. It's easy to get carried away when one starts growing, and it's quite surprising how quickly one will reach the limits of the structure. Another essential fact to consider is that the bigger the greenhouse, the fewer temperature fluctuations are experienced.

Tips for Choosing the Right Size Greenhouse

The size of a greenhouse structure will mainly be determined by the types and numbers of crops, plants, and other products that one wishes to grow. However, it's also equally important to note that it will require additional protection from the elements and the weather for plants to grow during the winter.

Typically crops that thrive in warmer weather could continue to grow all-year-round. Produce that requires an equal balance of cold and warm weather can be protected from harsh sunlight by installing a shade cloth.

So how does one determine the required square footage of your greenhouse? The best way to go about this phase of the process is to create a floor plan that includes

- growing areas
- storage spaces
- walkways
- workspaces

Remember that sufficient space should be calculated, so plants never touch the structure's walls. Plants that touch the greenhouse sides are exposed to the cold in winter and will not have access to the proper airflow circulation they need to grow. You should also plan accordingly to ensure that you can reach all plants from all sides to tend to them appropriately.

Greenhouse walkways need to handle human movement, equipment, and crops when going in and out of the structure. But, the key is limiting storage and walking areas to allow as much produce as possible. In a commercial greenhouse, the structure may have to accommodate different types of vehicles either inside or close to the greenhouse for loading and unloading purposes. This will also be a crucial planning point in ensuring that the doors and entrances to your structures can accommodate this.

If you are somewhat constricted in budget, the structure can be made smaller, and less expensive semi-permanent greenhouses can be used in certain growth stages. There's also the option to transplant bedding plants outside and protect them with temporary coverage.

It's relatively straightforward to repurpose the space inside a greenhouse application to gain larger production yields. For example, a frame made from metal or wood can be added over a supply area, instantly making room for more plants. You can also erect temporary benches between transplanted fruits and veggies, and then relocate them as the space becomes constricted. Regarding companion plants, crops like radishes, lettuce, and spinach can be planted between peppers and tomatoes as they will be ready for harvest before the latter and can be harvested before the plants compete with one another for resources.

The primary vertical supports or rafters of a greenhouse need to be high enough to allow the addition of hanging baskets and for the workers to stand up straight without bumping their heads. One consideration to take in this regard is to ensure that the rafters are spaced far enough apart to avoid overcrowding and resource competition.

If you are still unsure about the size of your greenhouse but keen to get started, it's a great idea to invest in a budget greenhouse that can be expanded at any time. Some greenhouses allow for extensions at the back, and the only other thing to consider is leaving some room at the back of the structure to allow for easy expansion.

What is the Average Size of a Greenhouse?

There isn't an average greenhouse size. There are simply too many determining factors, such as plants, preference, type, and backyard size. Typically a greenhouse hobbyist will invest in a structure between 6' x 4' and 10' x 20'. However, if a common size were recommended, the suggestion is to start with a size range of 6'x8' or 8'x10'. In the author's opinion, this is the ideal size boasting sufficient space to grow an array of crops.

The next greenhouse dimension to take into consideration is height. A typical hobbyist structure is at least seven feet tall to accommodate an adult standing up straight and creating enough room for plants. If you want to cultivate certain crops, a taller greenhouse is suitable. However, bear in mind the taller the greenhouse, the more heat it requires.

Typical Greenhouse Sizes

If you are a gardener who loves rooting and planting in the soil, space is your best friend. When you have to spend a significant amount of time on your knees, the thrill might quickly disappear, and with it, your motivation to grow your own crops. However, when it comes to seeds and smaller plants, they will eventually require more space to mature. Therefore, it's crucial to allow your plants plenty of room to grow and for you to be able to reach all the sides easily.

With a larger greenhouse, the price will naturally be higher and require additional watering and heating resources. So let's unpack the three different sizes of greenhouses and how they'll impact your budget.

Greenhouses can be divided into three different size categories:

- Small
- Medium
- Large

Small Greenhouses

As we've already established, no set size categorizes a greenhouse as small, medium, or large. As mentioned, a 6'×8' ft greenhouse is seen as small but still features sufficient space to move around and can harbor a solid amount of produce at any given time. This is a very popular size among greenhouse hobbyists and gives you plenty of greenhouse types to choose from. However, if you still find this size a little intimidating at first, you can also opt for the 6' x 4' alternative.

When you're constricted in terms of space, you can invest in a mini or indoor greenhouse of this size. It's a fun way to allow you to explore what it takes to grow your own herbs and veggies, before perhaps moving on to a larger structure.

Medium Greenhouses

The standard dimensions for a medium-sized greenhouse is typically 8'×12'. With these greenhouses, you have the chance to grow your own crops on a semi-professional level and the option to grow many different kinds of plants, all at the same time. This is an excellent solution if you have some time on your hands and capital to invest. In addition, it gives you the freedom to start small and then scale or expand later.

Large Greenhouses

This is the giant of greenhouses for the serious greenhouse fundis. A large greenhouse usually is 10 feet wide or larger. The biggest difference between a medium and a large greenhouse is the additional width and the ability to use more planting space. Large greenhouse applications range between 16-24 feet long and come with many different features. For example, some structures boast an internal partition and a door that provides two different growing spaces. This means that you can experiment with various plants and different growing climates. For example, tomatoes can be planted in warmer areas and other plants in cooler regions. Notably, big greenhouses will need a higher budget and more time. This is because the required labor will be time-intensive and require much more space.

CHAPTER 7:
GREENHOUSE FLOORING

Another question often asked is whether a greenhouse actually needs a floor. When you want to plant directly in the soil, your structure can be built directly on the ground. This option is great and naturally features adequate drainage. However, it's only recommended in areas boasting quality loam soil.

When you have muddy soil, you'll require flooring and a foundation to prevent the ground from turning into useless dirt after each watering session. Apart from this scenario, there's really no need for flooring if you use the raised bed approach in your greenhouse. You only need to cover the main path with gravel and construct raised beds on either side of the main path.

However, let's take a moment to explore the different options regarding greenhouse flooring.

The Different Types of Greenhouse Flooring

Bricks

It's important to note that brick flooring in a greenhouse can be equally as costly as a concrete floor. The two main differences are that a brick floor presents a more polished and aesthetically pleasing finish.

Brick greenhouse floors don't need an additional drainage system or mortar. This is because bricks can absorb water and increase the humidity inside a greenhouse.

In the instance of smaller greenhouses, you'd only need a single-skin bricklayer. And larger greenhouses would need increased stability; therefore, a double-skin layer will be sufficient.

Brick flooring doubles as a foundation and lasts for a long time, making it a great option if the funds are available.

Concrete

A layer of concrete doesn't merely serve as a foundation, but also as a type of flooring. It bears mentioning that using this material results in the most costly of floor types due to the cost of raw materials. In addition to the expense, you'd likely have to get a professional to install the floor.

However, if you can pay the price, this is a great long-term flooring option for your greenhouse. Not only is it durable, but it's also easy to maintain and can withstand most weights.

On the downside, concrete doesn't make for good drainage, but this can be mitigated by pouring the material at a slight angle.

Gravel

Gravel flooring is one of the most cost-effective options at your disposal. Installation is simplified by only using a plastic ground cover and adding gravel. Even though this is a cheap option, combining the two factors makes for a sturdy greenhouse floor. Furthermore, gravel flooring is effortless to maintain and prevents erosion by providing a barrier against rodents.

Gravel also increases drainage capabilities. A porous plastic ground cover sheet will also eliminate weed growth while promoting moisture seeping through the pores to where it's needed most.

One downside of gravel greenhouse flooring is that the gravel travels underfoot. This can be avoided by adding an edging material such as bricks or lumber.

Landscape Rocks and Pebbles

If you are looking for a DIY option that is also pleasing to the eye, adding pebbles and rocks to your greenhouse floor is your answer. Sadly, the cost of these materials dissuades most people from using them. Another consideration with landscape rocks and pebbles, is that you'll likely have to invest in additional drainage as the water builds up between the materials.

Lastly, this greenhouse flooring type is prone to weeds, so before laying the rocks and pebbles, the whole weed and its root systems need to be eliminated. Adding a weed mat or cloth can hamper further weed vegetation growth. After laying this mat, the rocks and pebbles can be applied on top.

Mulch

Mulch is another excellent option for greenhouse floors. It's sturdy, promotes drainage, and even improves soil quality. Mulch is a great greenhouse floor cover to consider when growing directly from the ground.

Mulch is cheap and prevalent in garden nurseries; however, it tends to break down and will need replenishing annually. The type of mulch that is most suitable for greenhouse flooring is shredded mulch. This material type interlocks, creating a sturdy and uniform walking platform. It's recommended to purchase mulch in cubic yards to make it more cost-effective.

Stone

This is another permanent greenhouse flooring option that is primarily mortared in place. The alternative is to use decomposed granite in between the stones to stabilize them, when they aren't mortared together. Greenhouse keepers often pair stone flooring with a surface drain to dispel surplus water.

The most common elements used for stone flooring in a greenhouse are flagstones or patio stones (also called stone slabs). Using these stones decreases the risk of falling or tripping when working in the structure. However, one type of stone that should not be used in this instance is fieldstone flooring since it's irregularly shaped, increasing the risk of injury.

Vinyl

There is a type of commercial vinyl flooring specially designed for greenhouse use. The most common materials used in the construction of this vinyl are polypropylene and polyvinyl.

Vinyl is a durable option, easy in terms of upkeep, and drains equally well. Some greenhouse vinyl flooring options are also anti-bacterial, anti-microbial, and even UV-resistant.

Weed Cloth

A weed cloth or a weed barrier is a woven fabric that prevents weed growth via the floor. Weed barriers are also level, meaning it's effortless to walk on. It also promotes drainage because water can seep through without the soil becoming too muddy.

CHAPTER 8:
GREENHOUSE FOUNDATIONS

Next on the list of considerations is the types of greenhouse foundations. By now, you've probably spent some time checking out photos of other greenhouse gardeners and possibly identified a sunny spot inside your structure for a cup of coffee as you admire your rows of beautifully growing crops.

Before you can reach that place of greenhouse zen, the most crucial tip I need to share with you is that it's imperative for the greenhouse's foundation to be square and level to ensure it's properly anchored. Greenhouse manufacturers take great care in producing structures and material that are square and genuine, and as such, it needs to be erected this way.

So what happens when a greenhouse application is not installed square and level? There are a range of issues one will experience to this effect, including the panel and frames not aligning and the door frame not fitting correctly, making it almost impossible to install.

That said, let's look at the types of greenhouse foundations.

Concrete Pads

If you're looking into investing in the most durable and practical greenhouse foundation from the get go, then a solid concrete base is your goto option. This foundation is ideal for large greenhouse applications and can easily be set above soil level.

Author's Top Tip

Keeping a concrete foundation well-maintained is an effortless task. It only requires a detergent washdown and a quick broom sweep to be kept in tip-top shape.

Pros

- Rodents can't tunnel through from the outside.

Cons

- You may experience standing water with this greenhouse foundation. This is because the water can only drain around the areas of a concrete base. However, this can be mitigated by drilling additional drainage holes in the concrete pad.
- This is one of the more expensive greenhouse base options, but the ease of construction makes it worthwhile. Adding expansion bolts also creates a more sturdy foundation.

Earth/Soil

If the greenhouse is installed on firm, well-compacted earth, the most straightforward (and budget-friendly) option is to lay concrete on each of the four corner frames and ensure the layer is level before the concrete dries.

Suppose you have identified an uneven area to erect your greenhouse. In that case, I'd recommend building the site up, making it more level using more soil, and compacting it down with a vibrating plate or a roller.

Author's Top Tip

It might be required that you support the frame in place as the concrete sets. However, this method is only recommended for greenhouses sizes 8ft x10ft or less. Any larger applications imply that the weight's frame will gradually push the foundation into the soil, especially after rain.

Pros

- Using a soil base and concreted leg posts suggests that you can plant directly into the ground inside the structure and ensure proper drainage and cost-effectiveness.

Cons

- With this method, there is a risk attached to the frame subsiding, causing the frame to warp and possibly the glass to break.
- The structure's inside can become muddy and waterlogged.
- Rodents can tunnel inside.

Paving or Slabs

This is probably one of the most aesthetically pleasing greenhouse foundations and one of the most practical. This base is crafted from paving blocks or paving slabs. It looks good, it's easy to maintain, and it's the ideal basis for pots or growing bags to be placed inside.

Author's Top Tip

If this foundation is laid correctly, it will serve its purpose for a long time. As with its perimeter base counterpart, this foundation can be fixed down using screws and plugs.

Pros

- Paving blocks or slabs will afford you an area that is easy to clean. You'd only need to disinfect it annually by washing it down.
- Excess water is easily drained away.
- The base won't subside or warp, providing that it is set well.

Cons

- This base is restricted as it can only harbor pots and grow bags.
- This foundation is more expensive than perimeter, earth and concrete bases.

Perimeter Base

The second greenhouse foundation option entails constructing a perimeter for the base of the greenhouse to rest upon. This solid perimeter can be made from concrete, breeze blocks, or paving slabs.

Perimeter bases can be erected above soil level, nullifying the need to dig the area before laying the base. However, blocks or slabs should always be set down firmly, using a concrete mixture that will allow them to solidify. I would also advise against laying slabs or blocks on the soil alone, eventually washing away, creating an unstable base.

No matter the approach, the base of a greenhouse should permanently be fixed to concrete or slabs, using screws and heavy-duty rawl plugs.

Author's Top Tip

I'd recommend sizing your base first before marking it out on the soil, using a material such as spray paint. This way, you can ensure that your base fits neatly on top.

Pros

The two main advantages of this foundation type are its cost-effectiveness and overall sturdiness. The middle part can be left as direct-planting ground or graveled to keep it looking neat since any stones will be held firmly in place via the perimeter base.

<u>Cons</u>

One drawback of this greenhouse foundation type is that it's pretty challenging to keep the foundation level during the construction phase and your measurements have to be on point.

Managing the Foundation Frostline

Before you even reach the greenhouse planning phase, I'd strongly recommend measuring all the parts needed for your home DIY greenhouse gardening kit (whether this is a project created from scratch or buying a ready-made greenhouse construction pack. This is because planning for a foundation will take compensation and adjustments for variations in the greenhouse components and shared walls.

The greenhouse base must extend below the frostline to ensure stability (typically four feet deep). Once the foundation heaves in windy conditions or settles, the structure's frame can twist, resulting in shattered glass.

Most patio slabs are poured four inches deep, sans footings, and therefore cannot support a greenhouse application. Should you wish to build on a slab, a digged trench below the frostline is required, then a concrete wall around the patio section, and lastly, setting the greenhouse on top.

It's also possible to erect a greenhouse on an existing wooden patio. However, the posts must rest on the footings (below the frost line). Other permutations around doing this include ensuring that the frames and posts are built from pressure-treated wood, and the deck needs to be made from cedar, pressure-treated lumber, or rot-resistant redwood. All of these wood elements can withstand humidity at its worst. A greenhouse erected on a pre-existing wooden deck will also require reinforcement directly underneath your structure with additional joists and posts resting on the footings below the frost line.

Greenhouse gardeners that have been in the game for a long time will definitely agree when I say that laying a greenhouse base is different in warmer weather compared to colder environments. This is why I mentioned the importance of ensuring the foundation is applied at least four feet below grade, which is below frostline. The reason is that the contracting and expanding of the soil with each freeze and thaw cycle in a year can weaken and ultimately shift the whole base. As a result, the entire greenhouse is at risk of collapse or damage when the floor is compromised.

Even though it's a complex undertaking, an existing damaged or weakened base can be fixed by reinforcing it with poles, rebar, or other supports and placing them as deep into the earth as possible. However, when starting from scratch, it's advisable to build on a not too shallow foundation.

Cold climate greenies have a different set of challenges compared to warm climate greenies. The good news is that each obstacle can be prevented and mitigated when one knows what to look out for. One of these issues that I want to unpack is insulating a greenhouse application.

How to Insulate Greenhouse Foundations

Greenhouse foundations built in growing climates featuring below-freezing temperatures will require insulation to protect the application during the frost-heaving season (spring).

Ensuring your greenhouse is insulated correctly will help your plants to flourish in the optimum growing conditions 365 days of the year. Let's look at my step-by-step greenhouse foundation insulation guide.

Step 1: Plan the greenhouse insulation before you lay the foundation

Once you've established the need for greenhouse insulation, you need to seek a foundation option that allows you to insulate the base efficiently and at minimum cost. In this regard, one material to steer clear of. Wooden foundations will cause aluminum corrosion in greenhouse frames once it becomes damp. In addition, insulating a wood base is ineffective as wood contracts and expands through the year as the temperatures drop and soar. Instead, I'd recommend using foam boards, sill plates, and solid plastic material.

Step 2: Lay out and level the base

Before continuing with your insulation endeavors, you'd need to seek an expert opinion on the depth of soil freeze in your area during winter. After obtaining the required information, you'd have a pretty good idea of how deep to dig your foundation (below frostline).

If you find that the depth is greater than 12 inches, you'd have to dig and create a supported foundation. This approach is where the plastic beams (made from plastic) rest on perimeter piers crafted from concrete. Start by measuring, compressing, and evening the base until it's level and square. Next, lay a layer of sand over the whole foundation (one inch deep). Then, add the area and perimeter piers and then the foundation beams. Next, move to the greenhouse floor and apply a spray foam insulator (polyurethane or polystyrene). Remember to leave a one-inch trench, approximately 12 inches deep, around the outer edge of the base.

Step 3: Adding the exterior sheets and greenhouse insulation

Move to the foundation perimeter next, and apply the foam insulation to the foundation, until it's square with the beam tops. Next, insert one-inch foam sheets around the outside of the foundation (inside the trench). Ensure that the sheets touch each other all the way around the outer edge. Next, add soil snugly around the sheets until they are firmly pressed against the perimeter beams.

Step 4: Attaching the greenhouse to the base

Start this part of the process by attaching the doors and frames of the greenhouse with large bolts and aluminum sill strips. Next, add the roof and install the glass or plastic panes.

Step 5: Install the interior floor of the greenhouse

Add a weed cloth over the entire floor area of your greenhouse before starting with the floor. Next, add your preferred floor material (options are mentioned above). For additional warmth, light-colored paving and white gravel can be added. This will reduce the need for artificial light sources. You can also consider adding concrete pavers, bricks, or lava rocks. These materials retain solar heat and create a warm environment inside the greenhouse application.

CHAPTER 9:
GREENHOUSE FRAMES

In order of importance, greenhouse framing takes second place before the design material. However, by no means does this imply that you should spend less time crafting a frame of inferior material or construction.

To achieve a frame that is wholly squared, one needs to build a proper frame from the get-go. Also, once the frame is in place, there's also the possibility of finding openings and cracks that might be hard to seal.

With greenhouse kits, you won't have any option on the material selection, but should you choose the DIY option, there is a range of materials to choose from. Let's look at the four available framing options and some pros and cons.

Aluminum

If you are looking for a low-maintenance greenhouse frame option, you might very well prefer to use aluminum. Aluminum is known for its ability to withstand elements by not breaking or rusting.

Unfortunately, this material is not very robust. Therefore, if one decides to use it in the construction of a greenhouse application, the support structures need to be doubled up for sturdiness by adding a material such as heavy-duty gauge parts.

On the upside, aluminum provides a solid frame for polycarbonate or glass panel installation. It can also be anodized or painted in colors of your choice.

Advantages

- **It's robust**: Aluminum is one of the most versatile construction materials. Not only can it withstand exposure to the elements, but it's also rust and rot resistant.

- **Can be scaled to size**: Aluminum can be scaled to any size and used in small, medium, or large greenhouse applications.

- **Sturdy and lightweight**: This material is light in weight but still strong enough to meet requirements.

- **Long shelf life**: Aluminum has an extended shelf life and looks great.

Disadvantages

- **Additional sturdy base must be purchased**: When buying a greenhouse kit made from aluminum, a greenie must note that it doesn't come with a sturdy base. Therefore this needs to be purchased separately. Aluminum greenhouse sites exposed to moderate to strong winds require a solid foundation to keep them from warping and bending.

- **Inability to retain heat**: Aluminum greenhouses require additional insulation due to their failure to keep out cold. With this drawback, it also means that with an aluminum structure comes the risk of condensation exposure, which needs to be mitigated.

- **High cost**: Because aluminum is a composite material, it comes at a high price. Because aluminum can bend and twist, it might be needed to use more of it than other material types.

- **Expansion difficulty**: It can be tricky to expand an aluminum greenhouse due to the thin frames and the material's cost.

Galvanized Steel

This material is durable and comes at a low cost. This is a great option, as it's not only strong but fewer frames will be needed, meaning fewer shadows are cast into your greenhouse application.

Most galvanized steel frames are compatible with polyethylene instead of polycarbonate or glass. Sadly, this combination is not very pleasing to the eye and might not be the ideal option for a home greenhouse enthusiast. Another consideration is that all steel eventually rusts and reaches a shelf life.

Advantages

- **It has the longest shelf life**: Not only is galvanized steel strong, but the actual material also takes a very long time to reach its expiration date.

- **It's robust**: Galvanized steel is the best option for withstanding heavy snow and wind.

- **Corrosion-resistant**: Because the material is non-corrosive, even home greenhouse enthusiasts that reside in seawater, and marine areas can use it for their structures.

- **Recyclable properties**: Galvanized steel is a recyclable material that can be reused, making it ideal for commercial and residential greenhouses.

- **Superior to wood frames**: This material is superior to wooden frames, as it's not prone to bending, twisting, or other deformities. All assembly pieces are square and uniform, making them an ideal choice for greenhouse applications.

- **Ability to withstand extreme elements**: Greenhouses made from galvanized steel can withstand harsh weather conditions and elements such as termites, earthquakes, and hurricanes.

- **No nails are required**: The galvanized bits for greenhouse frames come with studs that are effortless to install and can be customized.

Disadvantages

- **Galvanized steel is expensive**: Galvanized steel is costly, meaning your greenhouse construction costs will be higher than other framing materials.

- **Unfamiliarity in greenhouse applications**: You might find that some zoning officials and building codes don't make provision for this type of structure in residential areas. The reason is that using galvanized steel to build greenhouses is not as common as other materials. This means that one can quite possibly expect a delay in the whole permit process (if required).

PVC Plastic

A greenhouse frame crafted from PVC plastic pipes will be low in cost, easy to assemble, and portable. Even though it might not be as rigid as the other three materials mentioned, greenhouse experts are now starting to use metal supports in this framing type.

PVC permits less heat loss than galvanized steel, for example, by using walls made from polyethylene film. This is an ideal frame type for beginner and hobby greenhouses. Most greenhouse kits come standard with PVC plastic frames.

Advantages

- **Temperature retention efficiency**: PVC greenhouses can retain heat really well. This is a great framing material, especially if you plan to grow crops from seedlings.

- **Lightweight and flexible**: This material is easy to lift, transport, and manipulate, making for an easy greenhouse construction process. This also means that if the greenhouse should be moved to another area, it can be easily dismantled and erected again.

- **Expense**: PVC piping costs are much cheaper than other framing materials. This makes it an excellent choice for beginner greenhouse hobbyists that don't want to incur high startup costs.

- **Easy DIY project**: This can be a very fulfilling journey if you use PVC piping to build your greenhouse in your own capacity. Many readily available internet resources provide step-by-by step instructions and requirements on how to do this.

- **Durability**: PVC is a very durable material, which will last long. However, the exception is areas with strong winds, where it won't be as effective.

Disadvantages

- **Exposure to sunlight causes deterioration**: PVC plastic exposed to sunlight will deteriorate over time. The best way to mitigate this is to ensure that any PVC material used has been UV–treated; this will extend the life to at least 20 years.

- **Greenhouse frames should be large**: The PVC frames need to be big to compensate for the material's and frame's lack of stability.

- **It's an eyesore**: PVC is not a very pleasing material to look at. Not only that, but the material's inability to blend in with the natural surroundings will somewhat come across as a temporary–looking structure.

Wood

Although wood is one of the most aesthetically pleasing materials in greenhouse applications, sadly, it doesn't make for a very practical framing option. The only exception is if one is to craft a greenhouse from a pre-existing garden shed or sunroom.

Wood is straightforward to assemble into a frame and relatively easy to make. However, greenhouses are damp, wet spots, and most wood types will eventually rot and warp due to the moisture content.

However, if you are still keen on a wooden greenhouse frame, use a rot-and moisture-resistant variant. Some options include chemically treated wood (for outdoor use), redwood, or cedar. At the end of the day, no matter the wood type used, you will have to add a sealant coat every other year to extend the shelflife thereof.

When installing a wood greenhouse frame, materials such as polycarbonate or rigid glass will be used for solar panels.

Advantages

- **Bulkiness**: Due to its weight, wood can withstand elements such as snow and wind.

- **Part availability**: Replacements for damaged parts are readily available and easy to install.

- **Design flexibility**: Bigger and more intricate greenhouses can be crafted.

- **Acts as a natural insulator**: Wood can maintain warm temperatures and takes longer to cool down, which favors greenhouse applications.

- **Adding additional hooks**: Extra hooks can be installed, creating additional storage space.

Disadvantages

- **Regular maintenance**: Wood needs to be treated frequently with paints and preservatives to ensure it doesn't lose its structure or collapse.

- **Labor-intensive**: Because of the time-consuming upkeep involved, maintaining a greenhouse with a wooden frame takes a lot of time. And remember, time is money. With every bout of maintenance, plants will need to be moved out and in again.

- **Takes longer to construct**: Building a wooden greenhouse application takes time due to the number of manual labor involved.

- **Not recommended for use in termite-prone sites**: Wood can easily fall victim to termite infestations. One can apply termite deterrents to the material, but it's not a long-term sustainable solution. In perspective, the cost of a wooden greenhouse's upkeep is equal to some costs of constructing an entire greenhouse from scratch.

- **Chemical treatments are not recommended**: One also needs to consider that it's not advisable to treat your greenhouse structure with chemicals is not advisable. This is especially true where food produce is being grown. Toxins can get absorbed in the soil and taken up by the plants. As a result, the plants can die, posing a severe health risk for consumers.

- **Increased pest control measures**: Because wood attracts wood borers and other wood-loving insects, it will need to be treated against pets regularly, meaning increased maintenance costs in this regard. Also, where the areas are badly damaged, they need to be replaced frequently too, which is another cost to consider.

CHAPTER 10:
GREENHOUSE GLAZING

A big part of any residential or commercial greenhouse construction is the glazing (Also called the covering). As such, there are four main types of covering, namely:

- fiberglass
- glass
- plastic films
- polycarbonate

By now, you are probably asking, "Which one is best for my greenhouse?" There are many considerations to take when deciding on the best-suited greenhouse glazing in your scenario. Some factors include the climate, crops, and budget. It is important to note that each type of material has its pros and cons. Let's take a look at the available material options.

Fiberglass

The first greenhouse covering under the microscope is the frequently used fiberglass option. When comparing the cost, fiberglass is cheaper than polycarbonate and glass but costlier than polyethylene. What I can say is that due to the structural backing not being required, the price is lessened a bit further. Fiberglass can also withstand catastrophic weather conditions, making it ideal for areas such as Florida in the United States.

There are some cons to using this material. One disadvantage is that it's vulnerable to sun exposure. When it is overexposed to sunlight, the material fibers expand, reducing the light that seeps through to the greenhouse application. Secondly, UV–treated fiberglass only lasts as long as five years before breaking down. This material is just as combustible as wood, and there's still a risk attached to flames igniting, even after removing the ignition source. Therefore many greenies prefer not to use fiberglass due to safety concerns.

Glass

Glass is the best option if you're looking for the material with the best light transmission and a high thermal rating. The light distribution can be further enhanced by imprinting small patterns on the actual glass. Compared to the other three options (mentioned below), glass lasts long, is UV radiation-resistant and can withstand air pollution. Glass is also a non-combustible material.

The biggest disadvantage of using glass is the cost. Even though the panels are cheaper than polycarbonate, glass is heavier and requires additional support during construction. This makes the startup quite costly. Two other disadvantages associated with glass are the material is prone to hail damage and birds flying into the material. Lastly, cracked glass panels are a frequent headache when it comes to replacing them, which needs to be done as soon as possible to protect your crops inside the greenhouse.

Plastic Films

Due to its low startup cost, this is one of the most popular greenhouse covering options. It requires minimal construction materials, especially when using it in conjunction with a Quonset greenhouse. Heating costs can also be reduced by 40% when using two layers of polyethylene coating and adding an air space in between.

Other pros include that plastic film is an excellent sunlight diffuser, meaning intense light can seep through in the greenhouse application at canopy level. It also yields very few shadows due to fewer trusses and braces used during the construction. This makes it an ideal glazing material for first-timers.

One of the significant cons of this glazing material is its short lifespan. As time goes by, the air pollution and sunlight will weaken the material, rendering it brittle and prone to tear and shred. This can be mitigated by applying UV inhibitors but will need replacing every second or third year. So, in conclusion, this is great as a starter but will become more expensive compared to other materials in the long run.

Polycarbonate

Polycarbonate is more rigid compared to polyethylene. It's also the latest addition to the greenhouse glazing market. It's available in three different sizes of thickness, namely:

- corrugated single-layer
- flat layer
- twin-wall

In addition to the three different types, it also features bronze-colored panels for sufficient light diffusion (ideally suited to commercial and retail greenhouse applications). This material can be used in conjunction with Quonset greenhouses and boasts great flexibility. In addition, using the double–layered version will offer excellent heat insulation capabilities.

Polycarbonate glazing is very durable and has a better element-resistance against inclimate weather conditions than solid glass. Compared to polyethylene, this is the better option since it's not prone to UV damage and air pollution. This means polycarbonate covering can last a decade before replacement is needed.

Regarding product cons, polycarbonate tends to yellow or cloud over time, so light into the greenhouse application can go to waste. Even the double-layer polycarbonate can be susceptible to algae. Luckily this can be mitigated by taping the ends shut when the greenhouse is built. Unfortunately, the high price makes it costlier than polyethylene and glass, but its durability more than makes up for it; if one can afford it.

Humidity

Greenhouses are prone to fungal infections. Therefore a defense mechanism must be in place to create the optimal growing conditions for the highest crop yields. One way of controlling this is managing the humidity and temperature of the greenhouse application so water doesn't accumulate on the plant tissue.

Humidity is at its most prevalent during hours that take place after sunset. This is because the greenhouse covering becomes cold during the cooler nighttime temperatures, and plants radiate towards the cooler glazing. As a result, wetness occurs when the foliage or covering reaches dew point.

To mitigate this, an effective strategy is required to avoid the conditions created by dew point. Two strategies include

- decreasing the pace of cooling in plant radiation
- dehumidifying the air using condensation, desiccant dehumidification, or ventilation.

Let's now look at the latter three techniques in more detail below.

Condensation

Condensation occurs on the undercarriage of a roof that is cold. Initially, greenhouses consumed much energy but boasted dry conditions, perfect for dehumidifying/condensing a surface area. However, modern greenhouse applications feature screens or curtains with less dehumidifying capabilities and walls that have been glazed multiple times. These factors in today's structures imply that we control humidity with incredible difficulty.

Condensation also happens on the inside of compressor-based ACs and conventional refrigerants. Water condenses and drains away while air is pulled over the cold refrigerant coils.

Some of the difficulties experienced with this approach are that mold and bacteria culminate inside and create saturated conditions. This spreads across the greenhouse canopy as the air moves across the coils. Together with the intensity of electric energy in a refrigerant's compression, it means that there are limits attached to the appropriation of heat pumps and conventional ACs.

Desiccant Dehumidification

This method uses an approach where water vapor is mopped up by elements such as iodine (salt). Energy is then needed to dry or regenerate the desiccant. Agam, an Israeli company, has developed a liquid synergistic dehumidification setup that operates on the basis whereby transpiration and convection are connected to address and link the plant and greenhouse dynamic, promoting increased energy efficiency.

The required energy is then borrowed for desiccant regeneration, and the inactive heat is used for the regeneration and dehumidification processes. This is then distributed to the plant zone, balancing heat needs. This method then decreases the yearly demand for energy consumption in heating by 60% compared to the ventilation technique and offers increased humidity control.

Ventilation

The most commonly-used humidification control method is ventilation. However, it's the most energy-intensive and provides minimal effectiveness and control. Increased water vapor is obtained, heating the air. When the limit for humidity and temperature is reached, the air inside is replaced with drier, cooler air from outdoors utilizing exhaust fans or vents.

With ventilation, the coolant must be recouped with heat to control the temperature. Notably, it's this heating found underneath crops that prompts plant transpiration. Interestingly enough, approximately 40% of the energy is dispatched under the greenhouse roof to help govern the humidity level and is then transfigured into water vapor by the plant. In conclusion, a continuous pattern of heating and ventilating occurs, producing transpiration. This means that ventilation is very energy–intensive and brings about the restrictions of humidity levels required inside a greenhouse.

Irrigation systems

The crops inside a greenhouse are irrigated using water and then distributed to the produce. There are a range of different approaches used to supply water to the plants. Some methods include:

- booms
- fertilizer injectors
- drip tubes
- overhead sprinklers
- manually (by hand)
- mat irrigation
- sub-irrigation (adding water to the bottom of a pot or container)
- tapes, or
- a combination of all the methods mentioned above

In short, hand watering and overhead sprinklers tend to waste water and only wet the crop leaves, creating the perfect breeding ground for plant injuries and pests/diseases. Conversely, subirrigation and drip systems prove to be the best at controlling water disbursement and are the most efficient. Because the leaves don't become wet, it decreases the crops' risk of injuries and diseases.

Each method mentioned above has advantages and disadvantages, and some are more suited to certain greenhouse applications sizes and types. Let's take a look at these factors in more detail below.

Booms

A boom irrigation system comprises a series of one or more pipes with nozzles that distribute H_2O to the plants as the system moves over them. Some common ways water is dispatched in this approach include a cart rolling down the middle path or an overhead rail system. There are two types of boom irrigation systems;

DIY booms

The DIY boom irrigation system is based on the cart method mentioned in the previous paragraph. The first prototype in this regard was built using a lawnmower frame with a foldable double boom supported above the crops. The cart was then attached to a rail via an arm fixed on a pipe attached to the ground. This method implies that the cart can easily move to different greenhouse spots. Even though it doesn't provide uniform irrigation like a commercial power unit, it's definitely time-saving.

Commercial booms

Commercial boom systems operate on power units. It can run on both a single and double rail system suspended above the plants.

Control measurements and requirements

Controlling both of these boom irrigation systems requires an adequate water supply. The most straightforward method is to use a cycle timer or a time clock. This will ensure that the system operates at a predetermined time.

Both boom systems have a distinct disadvantage in that counter–measures must be implemented to manage issues such as power outages and low water pressure. Boom systems also feature significant advantages such as less water and fewer aisle space requirements.

Considerations

Many boom irrigation options are available, making the right choice an overwhelming endeavor. Factors include greenhouse type, size, and crop types. Therefore some time will be spent doing due diligence and deciding which option is best.

Recommended use

Boom irrigation works best with gutter–connected or free–standing greenhouse applications. Boom widths can reach up to 70 feet, meaning that bed lengths or benches of up to 400 feet can be irrigated simultaneously.

Fertilizer Injectors

These devices are used to apply nutrients such as mineral acids, pesticides, plant growth regulators, water-soluble fertilizers, and wetting agents to growing plants. Even though they are costly, they form an integral part of any greenhouse operation. The high cost can be justified by the simple and labor–saving solution this method supplies chemical solutions to greenhouse production.

This irrigation system features many promising benefits, but there is a high risk of the system malfunctioning, leaving ruined crops in its wake. This can be somewhat mitigated by applying regular maintenance checks and recalibration to ensure the system works at its best.

Considerations

There are many fertilizer injector types on the market, including:

- Anderson injectors
- Dosatron injectors
- DosMatic injectors
- EC and pH controllers
- Gewa injectors
- positive-displacement injectors
- Smith injectors
- venturi-type injectors

Again, a newbie greenie might have difficulty selecting the best option with so many options at your disposal. Some considerations to take before buying a fertilizer injector includes:

- Chemicals
- Greenhouse size
- Fertilizer injection rate
- Injector type
- Type of fertility program
- Stock tank size
- Water flow rate & calculation, and
- Water quality

Drip Tubes

The drip tube method is a valuable commodity in greenhouse gardening. It provides an accurate level of moisture control, reduces soil water pollution, and saves labor time.

Drip tube irrigation systems can also dispel the issue of water missing the pot during overhead irrigation, controlling the volume of water. Control is governed by utilizing a tensiometer that senses when the moisture level has reached capacity, by turning the system off.

The most common use for drip irrigation includes growing flowers and vegetable crops. These plants are typically watered by employing drip tapes. The tubing is then placed above the ground, woven through the bags, or placed on top of the plant containers.

Advantages

- A high availability of nutrients and water.
- The drip irrigation system dosage can be customized to match the plants' requirements.
- There is good soil aeration and no saturation involved.
- Access fertilizer application is decreased since the controlled method avoids high salinity.
- Leaves don't get wet, eliminating the occurrence of fungal diseases.

Disadvantages

- A time-consuming installation process.
- When the drip tubes are exposed to sunlight, they might deteriorate or break, requiring replacement.
- The plastic drip tubes can affect the fertility of the oil. In addition, the sunlight degrades the plastic over time, affecting the fertilizer and soil quality.
- Drip tubes can get clogged. Therefore regular maintenance checks are required. If left untreated, H20 won't be able to reach the plants, exposing the roots to dehydration.
- If the system is not installed correctly, wastage factors such as water, heat and time come into play.

Recommended use

Drip systems are best suited to medium-sized greenhouses. One tube is placed into each pot, which is connected to the main water supply, delivering uniform moisture levels to all plants. When the crops need moisture, the main water supply is turned on, the tubes are filled with H20, and moisture is then sprayed directed to the topsoil.

Drip irrigation can be automated or done manually. It conserves water by targeting the soil instead of the overhead leaves, eliminating foliage diseases.

Overhead Sprinklers

Overhead sprinklers, also called misting systems, are an automating overhead watering approach for greenhouse irrigation. It's predominantly used to purify the air from dust and increase humidity. This is an ideal solution for greenhouses where crops are grown from seedlings. It's a very precise and efficient irrigation method.

Misting systems boast significant advantages and features. First, it reduces the overall cost of running a greenhouse operation, meaning faster paybacks. This is one of the best irrigation methods that reduce stress on plants. The anti-drip design prevents plant disease and reduces injury to the seedlings. When it comes to constant moisture, you can be assured that your crops are thoroughly watered each time, boosting germination development. Lastly, overhead sprinklers require very little maintenance and are highly durable.

Notably, misting systems also have a few disadvantages. Some include a higher risk of wind drift and evaporation issues than drip irrigation systems. Overhead sprinklers also moisten both weeds and crops. I also won't recommend using misting systems for crops and plants prone to foliar diseases. Lastly, overhead sprinklers have a higher risk for erosion and runoff than the drip tube method.

Consideration

Even though a misting system saves mainly on time, it requires regular maintenance to ensure its functioning at an optimum level. They also work best for juvenile crops and seedlings when they are ready to be transplanted elsewhere.

Recommended use

Greenhouse operators with large greenhouses and commercial operations will benefit from overhead sprinklers or misting systems. This method comprises a series of water pipes installed under the greenhouse roof with nozzles at certain space intervals. Each nozzle dispatches a fine mist across the top of the leaves, promoting even H20 distribution throughout the whole application.

Greenhouse misting systems are available in automatic and manual variants, which are budget-dependent. In addition, each individual nozzle can be configured at a different angle, ensuring the mist reaches the intended target.

Manually

A DIY or manual irrigation application implies watering greenhouse crops with sprinklers, nozzles, and hoses by hand. These systems have minimal startup costs compared to an automatic system but require more time to operate. However, this might not be a bad thing, as hand watering can be a soothing chore to some.

Another pro associated with manual irrigation systems implies that while one hand waters the crops, it means that the plants can be closely inspected for any issues before becoming a bigger problem.

Conversely, some cons include that the system can't be automated, implying the labor and time-intensive tasks can be ineffective to some and harder to train staff on how to get the moisture volumes just right. In addition, with manual irrigation, it can be hard to keep the plant's canopy dry, increasing the risk for fungal diseases. Finally, hand watering is also a precise science in that the water flow must be controlled at all times to ensure that the soil's structure isn't compromised. But, again, this implies that manual systems can be largely wasteful.

Considerations

Plants must be inspected before each irrigation session, and each pot or container's weight must be carefully assessed. Merely checking the plant at face value won't accurately estimate whether additional moisture is required.

There is an increased risk of overflowing the plant container, which will disrupt the soil structure and will force some nutrients to settle at the bottom of the container. This implies that drainage and dry down cycles will be compromised.

Recommended use

Manual irrigation systems are best-suited to hobbyist, backyard, or small–scale farming operations. This method is also an excellent choice for urban greenhouse farmers living in arid and dry climates where water scarcity is a genuine concern. It affords the small fry farmer the opportunity to grow farm-to-table produce using the available techniques.

Capillary Mat Irrigation

This method comprises installing a mat system and placing the plant containers on top. The water features a nutrient-rich solution. There are several sizes of capillary mats available, ranging in sizes from ¼–½ in thickness. This mat is placed on a level bench on top of a plastic layer. H20 is then fed from the plastic tubes atop the fabric.

Algae is controlled by installing a layer of perforated plastic film on top of the capillary mat, in addition to adding algicides. Some greenhouse keepers tend to turn the mat over with every new plant cycle. Plant containers must be enclosed in black film or painted black to decrease the risk of algae formation and excessive light. This will also ensure the piping and nutrient solutions remain intact.

Advantages

- Many plant species and sizes can be placed on the same fabric stretch. This ensures that no plants are over or underwatered.
- Option of adding more containers at leisure without the risk of evaporation loss.
- Reduced concerns of pests, since the floor stays drier.

Disadvantages

- Mats require constant, heavy watering.
- Containers need to be in constant contact with the mat.

Using this method can result in cost-saving and proliferating crops of uniform size without worrying about foliar diseases. This method of bottom watering develops robust root systems without injuring the crops. Capillary mat systems reduce associated pest concerns as minimal standing water surrounds the produce, meaning the greenhouse films remain drier.

Considerations

With this irrigation method, flat-bottomed containers need to be placed on the mat. These pots must be saturated before mat placement to ensure adequate water uptake. The mat needs to be soaked continually and should be in constant contact with the containers to draw the H20. However, if the pots are disturbed, this system will be rendered ineffective, implying that the containers must be re-watered from the top to put the capillary action back in motion.

Subirrigation

Subirrigation is also referred to as seepage irrigation. This method of watering plants consists of H20 being delivered right to the plant's root zone.

Advantages

- Less labor-intensive operation that promotes uniform crop growth.
- Less water, fertilizer, and other chemicals are needed, meaning costs can be saved.

<u>Disadvantages</u>

- Needs to be monitored constantly to ensure everything is in working order.
- Not suitable for plants requiring coarse soil.

Considerations

Before installing seepage irrigation, some factors to consider include your available budget, water supply, energy sources, and how much time you'll have for maintenance issues. Seepage irrigation only wets a small spot at a time. This can prove difficult for plants that don't like to grow in softer soil.

Tapes

This system comprises a pipeline with the added feature of drippers located inside the tubes. The tubes are made of a thin wall of about eight millimeters. The drippers are then evenly spaced out within the tube.

Tape irrigation is an excellent option for seasonal crops planted in a row. This system is for low-pressure and low-flow applications.

Advantages

- Extremely water efficient
- Water distristribution can be controlled
- Works best on level ground

Disadvantages

- Tedious to install
- Tubes will deteriorate over time
- Tubes can get clogged if not flushed regularly

Considerations

One of the biggest drawing cards of the tape irrigation system is its water efficiency. Greenhouse enthusiasts will benefit more, as the application suits structures erected on level ground. The greenhouse keeper also has improved control at their disposal, as the water distribution can be controlled.

Unfortunately, this irrigation system will require some patience and time to install. Furthermore, the environmental elements eventually take their toll on the tubes that will require replacement. Lastly, there is also a high probability that the pipes will get clogged over time, meaning water cannot seep through, and plants will dehydrate.

Questions to ask yourself before investing in this irrigation include: Is there sufficient water supply at all times? Do you need or want plant zones? Which is better: a drip tape or a drip line?

Combined Irrigation Systems

This practice combines two or more irrigation applications discussed above in your greenhouse structure. Commercial greenhouse gardeners would use various irrigation techniques in most cases.

But with so many options, which greenhouse irrigation system is best for me?

Factors That Determine the Best Greenhouse Irrigation System

There's no denying that all gardeners enjoy a gratifying sense of peace when hand watering their plants. However, time is everyone's enemy. With the increased demands of life chomping away our time to do what we love most, we have to consider alternative options.

Most serious greenies will lean towards using one or more of the irrigation systems mentioned above, to ensure ample return on their investment. So, with so many different types of irrigation, how do I choose the best one? I can tell you that the two main factors that influence your choice will be the number of plants and the size of your greenhouse application. Therefore, let's look at the best irrigation options for the three typical greenhouse sizes.

Small

Lean-to or window-based greenhouses provide sufficient space to cultivate several different crops without investing in additional irrigation systems. For example, mat irrigation is an ideal option for greenhouse gardeners looking to keep only a small garden space. These mat systems provide a uniform and consistent supply of water from their tubing. So your plants will be just fine, even when you can't inspect them daily.

Medium

For medium-sized structures, drip tubing is your best option. You can place one tube into each pot, and the main tube will be connected to the main water supply. Here, you also choose between a manual or an automatic timer device to deliver water to the plants when needed. It's also great for conserving water since the tubes are placed at the soil base. In addition to its water-preserving properties, this irrigation system also decreases the risk for plant diseases.

Large

An overhead irrigation system would be best practice for the more serious gardener or the greenie that wants to go bigger. They are ideally suited to larger or commercial operations and can be configured manually or automatically, meaning this is a budget-friendly option.

Plant-Specific

If you want to use the space to cultivate plants with different watering requirements, such as succulents, you might want to invest in a perimeter irrigation system. Perimeter applications operate on the premise of dividing your shelves, starting with plants that require the most to the least amount of moisture. This way the plants that need watering most often will get their fill, and the plants that don't need moisture will benefit by getting water when needed.

Location

It seems like a simple enough choice to make, right? Wrong! Again, by now, I'm sure you've realized that greenhouse gardening is a much more complex undertaking than initially anticipated. Therefore the following consideration to take would be the placement of your greenhouse structure.

Before you decide on the prime spot for your application, you'd have to establish what you plan on growing inside the structure and the type of greenhouse you'd like to erect. As we've already established, if you are a greenhouse hobbyist, the chances are that you won't go bigger than a small to medium size greenhouse. On the other hand, if you plan on building a greenhouse for commercial purposes from the get-go, you'll most likely look for a larger-sized structure.

While the greenhouse's stature determines its location, so does the crop type. One of the first factors to consider in both instances is the amount of sun exposure the plants need to grow. However, also bear in mind that plant-dependent, some plants may require afternoon shade.

The location of your greenhouse will dictate the structure type and the intensity and direction of the sun it will be exposed to. Other factors to consider here are the ability of the said structure to withstand exposure to harsh elements and the amount of free time (plus budget) you can spend on maintenance when required.

With the sun exposure in mind, it might be necessary to invest in additional heating sources such as fossil fuels to control the greenhouse temperature. Some applications can be placed against a basement, door, or window, which can emit and disperse heat to the greenhouse. But, this might prove too costly for you compared to heating the greenhouse separately when required.

The general rule of thumb is erecting a greenhouse on the south or southeast of a property or house. This spot is exposed to the most sunlight during the fall and winter seasons. If this is not an option, the east (first alternative) or southwest and west sides (second and third options) are the best. The north side should only be used as a last resort.

Furthermore, it's wise to place the greenhouse (lengthwise) from north to south. This supplies the application with more light compared to shade. This is perfect for crops that require morning light and afternoon shade. Other placement options include placing the structure near deciduous trees to protect the crops from scorching summer temperatures and provide adequate light in fall months (due to the leaves falling). However, be aware of falling sap, leaves, and branches.

Lastly, ensure the building site is level and the ground drains well. Don't build the structure near a sloping base or at a spot where cold air is transformed to frost in the winter months.

Temperature control

By now, some of you might be curious as to how one can extend the growing season. The simplest way of achieving this is by controlling the temperature. Controlling the climate inside your greenhouse consists of two factors:

- heating
- cooling

Ways to Heat a Greenhouse

A greenhouse gardener has the option of extending a growing season by a few months annually. Some even get away with growing crops all year long, without the addition of a heating system.

However, in most climates, the nighttime winter temperatures are too cold for most crops. It is here where greenhouse hobbyists would add heating systems. The three most common heating systems are:

This greenhouse heating type is the most efficient of the three options. It's known that electric heating provides 100% efficiency (Tip #7: Grow All Year Round with Affordable Heating Options, n.d.). Sadly, a significant drawback of this heating system is the associated costs, which might be too expensive for the average greenhouse hobbyist.

Luckily there are specific ways to supplement heat naturally to help alleviate the cost burden. One way is to use passive solar heat. If you decide to install an electric heater, I'd recommend investing in a 240V one with adequate heat capacity. In the long run, these units save costs and are reliable.

There's also the option of going with a 120V unit, but only the types that actually heat the air. The best affordable 120V heaters are the radiator oil-filled type. These heaters can provide the required heat for a small greenhouse application when placed near a fan.

Gas

This is the most cost-effective option, making this the preferred choice of greenhouse hobbyists worldwide. However, one precaution to consider is avoiding using open flame heaters. These gas heaters emit ethylene gas which is harmful to budding plants such as orchids. Another drawback of open flame heaters is their safety oxygen sensors that automatically switch the unit off when the oxygen levels are depleted inside the greenhouse.

Most modern greenhouses are virtually airtight, implying that oxygen levels are quickly depleted. If the heater turns off at night, the crops inside the greenhouse could die. Therefore, the best gas heater option would be those that are power exhausted and feature a flu.

Greenhouse gardeners need to make a hole into the greenhouse's side to serve as an exhaust. Overall, greenhouse gas heaters provide an 80% energy efficiency (Tip #7: Grow All Year Round with Affordable Heating Options, n.d.).

Passive solar heat

This method occurs when the heat of the sunlight is collected during the day and then released at nighttime when it's colder. This is done with H2O or a type of thermal mass that can absorb and retain heat for some time.

One way of doing this is to line the north wall of the structure with black water containers. These containers then absorb the light and slowly release it into the greenhouse application when the temperature drops.

This system can be combined with electric heat, significantly reducing annual heating costs.

Sustainable Greenhouse Heating Sources

Technology is simply marvelous, and each of us is responsible for seeking new and innovative ways to use sustainable energy sources in our daily lives. As such, here are seven alternative methods to heat a greenhouse.

- Biomass heating
- Ground to air heating
- Hot water heating through solar heating panels (hydroponic heating)
- Livestock heating (adding a chicken coop to the greenhouse)
- Making hotbeds with composting materials
- Renewable electricity heating
- Rustic heaters (using candles and plant pots)

For a greenhouse to function at its best, it requires a ventilation system that gives cooling, removes humidity, and allows for air mixing. There are two ways to achieve this, natural ventilation or fan ventilation. Let's take a look at each in more detail.

Fan ventilation

- Maintenance is one of the most essential factors with fan ventilation. Fan belts should be checked often to detect tension and wear before it becomes a more significant issue. A squeaking fan would be one of the first audible signs that the belt is worn out. Clean fan blades will increase airflow, and shutters need to be lubricated.

- Redirecting air circulation from the fan flow. The best approach is positioning the HAF fans to blow from shutter to fan end. This method ensures the air is pushed along faster, providing increased cooling. However, it might imply that you must reverse the airflow direction of one row of fans. It's crucial to seal all cracks and close all doors so that the air travels from the shutter intakes to the fans, providing maximum airflow.

- Staging fans are excellent for cost–saving measures. Using thermostats or electronic controllers, fans can be switched on when the temperature rises. The most energy-efficient fans boast small motors with large diameters. The best practice is to replace 1 and 1.5 horsepower motors with NEMA premium motors.

They are also 86% efficient and use eight to ten percent less energy than standard motors (J. Bartok, 2019).

- Keep insect screens clean by spraying water from the inside. The ideal pressure drop in the house should equal less than 0.1 inches of water (in static pressure when measured with a manometer). This will prevent the structure from overheating.

- Using evaporative cooling, you can control the structure temperature to several degrees below the outside ambient temperature. Portable evaporative coolers are effective for this application and are effortless to install, with minimal maintenance requirements.

Natural ventilation

- Greenhouse cooling can quadruple by coupling side vents and roof vents. In the case of freestanding structures, vents should be present on both sidewalls and ridges. During installation, the leeward vents should be installed to create a vacuum at the ridge's apex. To achieve the best results, I would advise that the combined ridge vent area and combined sidewall vent area equate to at least 20% of the floor area.

- Opening doors will allow more air to enter the greenhouse; the more air inside the greenhouse, the better the cooling. Natural ventilation provides uniform air, but this alone will not cool the structure to a cooler temperature than the outside ambient air.

- Open weave interior shade screens allow hot air to dissipate uniformly via the house. Crack-closed weave screens can be used as an alternative but could result in uneven crop growth as the sunlight will only seep through certain plant canopy parts.

- When using natural ventilation, ensure the HAF fans are switched off. It will increase energy use, resulting in a high electricity bill, and will also counteract the airflow ventilation.

- Lastly, skirts can be added to roll up sidewalls. Creating a plastic strip between 12 and 24 inches high will keep cold drafts out and protect ground-grown crops.

Wind securing

If you reside in a heavy windy area, securing your greenhouse is one of the most important precautions to take. The first thing that bears understanding is that once wind reaches inside a greenhouse, it will stop at nothing to get back out again. It also seldom exits how it entered. In the case of greenhouse applications, as more air seeps through the structure, pressure builds up, and this is when panes are blown to shreds, and parts like glazing clips pop off.

A missing glass pane is one of the obvious ways for wind to gain entry to your structure. Cracked glazing can be fixed temporarily with a glazing repair tape but must be replaced as soon as possible. In addition, I would strongly recommend doubling up on W-clips for all the glass frames and adding a silicone sealant to secure the clips in place for an added strength factor.

One of the most secure options is to fit the panes with bar caps. Although these fixtures might not be compatible with all the greenhouse types, glazing repair tape can be used on the interior and exterior to tape the overlapping panes together. Furthermore, inspect the corners of the frames. In the majority of the cases, the structure doesn't meet the corner 100%. These gaps can be filled with a silicone sealant for a permanent solution.

Furthermore, ensure the structure's door has a safety catch or a lock to ensure it shuts securely. A brick can also be wedged against the door to prevent it from flinging open.

Any rubber glazing strips around windows, doors and vents should be inspected regularly and should be replaced as soon as it's necessary. Doors, vents, and windows should close in a snug manner. From personal experience, I can advise that applying foam strips of anti-hotspot tape around my windows, doors and vents will prevent rattling and provide an increased sealing solution.

In worst-case scenarios, an entire greenhouse application can become airborne from strong winds, especially those with polycarbonate glazing. This can be avoided by ensuring the greenhouse is properly anchored. I recommend bolting the structure to a metal base that rests on the soil but a foundation that is deeply concreted at each corner. So far, mine has never moved, and this appears to be an effective solution.

Some other precautions to take include:

- Securing the greenhouse with anchor stakes or fixing pegs.
- Covering and burying extra greenhouse material in trenches.
- Making use of reinforcement patches.
- Securing the greenhouse to a sturdy fence structure.
- Placing paving slabs around the greenhouse base.
- Loading the bottom shelf with slabs of paving.
- Erecting the structure in a sheltered location.
- Taping the spot where the metal frame and PVC meet.

Now that you've garnered a good idea of all the different factors that bear consideration when erecting a greenhouse, the next question that is often asked is "Should I craft a greenhouse from scratch, or should I buy a ready-made greenhouse kit?" Let's explore both of these options in more detail.

Building vs. Constructing a Greenhouse

The first option we'll unpack in this chapter is constructing a greenhouse from scratch and all the required steps needed to build the structure of your dreams.

A Step-By-Step Guide on Constructing a Greenhouse

There are many ways in which you can build a greenhouse. For example, a small structure can be erected from a ready-made kit, which you can find online at any nursery or hardware store. Alternatively, you can craft your own attached or free-standing application. Your greenhouse flame and covering will dictate the types of tools and materials required. Here is a general overview of what you can expect to use.

- **Extras:** This includes gravel, poured concrete, glue, sealant and a measuring tape.
- **Greenhouse covering:** Whatever material you decide on must trap heat and protect your growing crops. Options include polycarbonate panels, glass or polyethylene sheeting.
- **Hardware types:** Standard hardware to have handy includes a drill, drill bits, screws, and nails.

- **Materials for building:** Pick a material to build your greenhouse frame based on your requirements. As discussed in the previous chapter, typical materials include aluminum, PVC pipes, and wood. You must do some due diligence to determine the desired durability, sturdiness, climate, and environment. For example, an aluminum frame is expensive, but you'd be assured that it's rust and precipitation resistant.

- **Tools for cutting.** Again, this will depend on the material you plan to use. For instance, a miter saw will be needed for cutting wood, and scissors will come in handy for cutting plastic sheets.

Now that we've listed the suggested tools and accessories let's look at the steps to take when building your own greenhouse.

How to Build a Greenhouse

There are various methods to building a greenhouse. This will depend on the available space and your budget. To make your own application, follow the steps below.

1. **Find your greenhouse plan.** There are many free plans available online for every type of greenhouse. I've also decided to add ten greenhouse plans to the book. It's crucial to find a plan as a reference framework before starting. This will then determine the tools required.

2. **Identify the greenhouse location.** Select a site for your structure that receives the most exposure to sunlight. It's advisable to ensure that the longer sides of the greenhouse face the east and west to obtain the most sunlight. I would advise against erecting your greenhouse near clusters of evergreen trees as these may cast shadows on certain crops, depriving them of the required sun. Lastly, ensure that the chosen spot allows for adequate drainage.

3. **Measure out the greenhouse structure.** Make use of a tape measure to measure precisely the amount of ground space your application will require. Ideally, this should be done before you select your greenhouse plan. This will ensure that you have sufficient space for your chosen design.

4. **Obtain the necessary permits.** Next, inquire from your local zoning office or municipality about whether any permits are required to erect the structure on your property. And when the building process starts, ensure that all local ordinances are adhered to.

5. **Select your foundation.** If you plan to build your greenhouse on uneven ground, a foundation will be required to stabilize the application and ensure it's draining correctly. For example, cold-climate gardens need the foundation to be laid beneath the frost line. However, if you prefer not to lay a foundation, you can apply landscaping fabric or create a well-drained floor with gravel.

6. **Construct the greenhouse frame.** Put your greenhouse frame in place, making use of the greenhouse plan. This includes cutting the material into the desired lengths and putting the entire structure together with the appropriate hardware and extras mentioned above.

7. **Covering the frame.** Use your selected greenhouse covering and cover the frame. Check for any holes, cracks, or leaks, and seal this with a silicone sealant to ensure it's adequately insulated.

8. **Ventilation.** The greenhouse's atmosphere should replicate the natural growing environment of plants. This includes proper ventilation and sufficient air circulation. This will prevent the application from overheating and falling victim to mildew and plant-based disease. Roof vents and circulation systems should also be installed to ensure the structure is adequately aerated.

Buying a New or a Used Greenhouse

Used Greenhouses

Investing in a used greenhouse is a great way to save money while having your own crops year-round. However, when considering going the route of buying a preloved greenhouse, five factors need to be taken into consideration. These are condition, covering, materials, price, and size.

Condition

You should ensure that the used greenhouse being bought is in good condition. Two types of warning lights include checking for cracks and/or rust in the covering and frame. These are telltale signs that the structure has had some wear and tear, meaning you won't get a prolonged lifespan from it. It also implies that you'd have to spend money sooner rather than later to replace the parts. Therefore, properly investigating the interior and exterior before purchasing a used greenhouse is crucial.

Covering

It's best to try and avoid glass, as it can be challenging to retain heat, and naturally, glass is prone to breaking. Plastics such as polyethylene film and polycarbonate sheeting are best as they involve minimal upkeep and are shatter-resistant. With the plastic materials mentioned, they come in varying levels of thickness.

Materials

As we've learned earlier in the book, there are many different types of greenhouse materials, and no one option is better than the rest, as they all come with their own pros and cons. However, aluminum or galvanized steel is best if you are looking for a premium, long-lasting option.

Price

On average, you can expect to pay between 25–70% less than the retail value for a second-hand greenhouse. But make sure that you look at several options in person before making your final decision.

Size

Pick a greenhouse size that can house all your plants and where you can stand upright while tending the crops. Taller greenhouses can retain heat better in winter and ventilate better in summer.

New Greenhouses

Similarly, with new greenhouses, there are five main factors to consider, this includes:

Brand reputation

Do your homework and ensure you buy a greenhouse kit from a reputable manufacturer. Some questions to ask include:

- Is there a warranty or guarantee offered? If so, what is the number of years, and which issues are covered?

- Is the company a household and trusted name? How many kits have they sold previously?
- Check previous reviews. Do the packages arrive in good condition?
- Does the manufacturer offer after-sales assistance once the product has been delivered? Are sales representatives available for installation and other product-related questions?
- Where is the product made?

Design and insulation

This will all depend on the climate where you'll erect your greenhouse. In other words, how cold are the winter months? *Glazing*

There are three main types: clear, opaque (diffused), and semi-opaque. The type of glazing you choose will impact the strength of the sunlight that will reach your plants.

Permits

Do you require zoning and/or other permits before erecting your greenhouse? Do you want a visually appealing option or more on the practical side?

Size

Ask yourself the question, do you envision a grower or a starter greenhouse? If you are looking for a relatively small starter-type greenhouse, you can simply add a bench and some seeds and you'll be ready to go (or is it grow?). Or is it that you want to start producing crops on a larger scale from the get-go? Then you'll require a grower-type greenhouse.

Whatever your needs, there is a greenhouse option for you that will allow you to have farm-to-table goodness at your fingertips.

Where to Find Used Greenhouses

There are many groups on social media, such as Facebook and Facebook Marketplace, Alibaba, eBay, and Amazon, where you find used greenhouses in good condition. However, use the guidelines above before investing in a secondhand structure.

Tools Needed to Disassemble a Greenhouse

Dismantling a greenhouse can come across as being an easier feat compared to reassembling one. However, bear in mind that this can become tricky at some point. One advantage is that fewer materials are required to disassemble a greenhouse than to build one.

Basic tools include:

- 10 or 11mm (0.39 or 0.43 inch) open-ended spanner
- Thin-bladed screwdriver
- Container to place the screws and fasteners in
- Ladder or portable steps

- Pair of heavy-duty gloves
- Eye protection (safety goggles)
- Protective headgear such as a hard hat

How to Disassemble and Transport a Greenhouse (plus precautions)

Working from the top down

It's best to start working from the top down. Start by removing any glass from the building's roof. If possible, have a second or third pair of hands on standby to assist with this stage. Glass panes can get heavy and be dropped easily, increasing the risk for damage and injury.

Next, remove the glass from the sidewalls before dismantling the greenhouse frame.

Rebuilding a greenhouse

If the plan is to relocate the greenhouse to a different spot, keeping certain frame parts intact is advisable. For instance, the roof slopes can be saved as one part. This will require a vehicle with a large roof rack to accommodate the dimensions in question.

There's a benefit to this, meaning if one takes down less of the greenhouse, there'll be less to rebuild once the new destination has been reached. But, on the other hand, it will require more labor and workforce. The drawback of this method is the risk of the frame bending while it's being transported and moved. However, the chances are you'll be less confused when reassembling the greenhouse with fewer bits and pieces at your feet.

Removing the clips

Investing in the right tool for this purpose will save time and frustration. There are many different clip types, but most look and function the same, meaning the same technique can be applied during the removal process.

Gently insert the blade of a screwdriver underneath each clip and lever it upwards bit by bit to avoid possible damage. Remember to keep one finger over each clip to prevent it from flying off, getting lost, or causing human injury.

Precautions to take with slippy glass

You might very well find that the glass panes might have a slimy appearance. Therefore, it's best practice to ensure that heavy-duty gloves are always worn. This grimy film is not always visible, and rust may also have affected joints and clips.

These factors can present issues if not handled with care and patience. This can be mitigated by running the screwdriver's blade along the edge of the overgrown moss and removing it. Ensure that the glass panes are clear of clips before handing them over to the next person.

Before removing the panes (especially in the case of different glass sizes), make a diagram with the measurements and some notes. This might take some time but will greatly help once the greenhouse is reassembled.

When moving onto the glass of the greenhouse sidewalls, always start by tipping the top edge out first and then lifting the pane outward so it's parallel and flat to the ground. This will decrease the chances of dropping a pane once it's free.

Remember that the sidewall panes will always be moved from the inside to the outside of the greenhouse and never from the outside to the inside. Similarly, with roof panels, they are pushed upwards towards the outside and not vice versa. With this in mind, it's a good idea to clear the immediate area around the greenhouse to avoid damage and injury during the dismantling process.

Transporting glass

The glass panes should always be securely strapped during the transportation phase. Old t-shirts, blankets, and tea towels are great tools to place between the panes to decrease the chance of them breaking.

It's advisable to place the panes of glass on the edge instead of laying them flat on the floor. This will ensure that each pane only has its own weight to support, instead of the bottom glass pane having to bear the burden of the full weight.

Remember that glass is more robust on end than when laid flat on the floor. Furthermore, ensure that the panes can't tip or slide. If possible, move the glass panes in the boot of a vehicle or the back of a van instead of the passenger sides.

Vents and doors

After all the glass panes have been removed, and the glazing has been stored, it's time to remove the structure's door. Start by taking the bracket off that stops the door from sliding. The door should now easily slide off its track. In the case of a hinged door, the bolts and pins need to be removed first (start from the bottom and work your way up). The door should now be able to lift outwards.

The next step in the process is to remove the roof's vents. They should slightly lift and be slid out along the side of the roof and out at the ends. Again, be aware that dirt particles trapped in the rooflines might make this task challenging, but some gentle wiggling should do the trick. You might also come across stoppers that prevent the vent from moving about. In most cases, the stoppers can be removed by taking the screw out that holds them in place.

In the case of automatic openers, these also need to be removed before any vent moves. They are also screwed in place, so they should be easy to remove with a screwdriver.

Next on the list are the slam bars. These features are held in place with two bolts. The bolts either need to be loosened or removed entirely in some instances. Then, slide the sidebars down, one by one, until it moves away from the corresponding glazing bar.

If you find that the bolts are corroded, take special care, as the chances are that other bolts might be rusted as well, meaning they will only come off with great effort. The alternative is to leave this section intact, but again there's a risk of bending and damage during transportation. Again, this is an issue as it might be challenging to find replacement parts.

Frame and roof

The next part to tackle is the roof bars. This is achieved by loosening the bottom and top bolts. This should be a straightforward task in most cases unless screws were used. If this is the case, it might prove challenging to remove, and it might be possible that a new bar would have to be purchased. This is not a big deal since most roof bars are interchangeable. Slowly loosen and remove the glazing bars one by one. If the bolts are corroded, tighten them instead, allowing them to rather break away.

Then, remove the bolts on each end of the ridge bar. The bars should now be able to slide out without issues. Because the bar is long, it's advisable to have a second pair of hands for this process.

The next part to remove should be the walls. Start by loosening the walls at the base. Because each greenhouse is different, there's no one-size-fits-all piece of advice on how to remove them correctly. But once the walls are removed from the greenhouse base, you should only be left with the bolted corners.

This is also tricky to explain, but loosening the bottom bold and sliding it away from the junction is the best start. Remove the top nut, allowing you to remove the roof corner support bar. Next, slide the bolt up and out via the junction. Now, the sidebar should be free to move out. Then, remove the top part of this section.

The next step is to remove the bottom junction as per the exact instructions above, except that there is only one bolt. Again, have a helper on hand since the structural integrity of the building will now be compromised.

Next, free up one side wall at a time, and set it down safely before continuing with the next one. Here it's recommended to have a few extra helpers on hand. For example, one person can move the wall away, and the others can hold up the other walls that are now unstable.

If possible, try to move the sections mentioned above while still intact. But if further dissembling is required, make notes, sketches, and take pictures first. You can even go as far as marking the sections with a sharpie.

When you're ready, you will re-erect the structure again by following the same steps for dismantling, but in reverse. However, first, ensure the base and assembly is square-shaped. The angles need to be precise otherwise, the square glass panes won't fit snugly together, and you'll have great difficulty assembling the greenhouse again.

Another significant factor is to ensure that the base is level and that the gutters are parallel with the foundations. You know what they say about a good foundation…

Moving on, let's look at all the factors when buying a ready-made greenhouse kit.

Buying a Greenhouse Kit

What is a Greenhouse Kit?

This package contains everything you need to build a hobby greenhouse. These kits boast various designs and sizes and come at different price tags suited for every budget.

Investing in a greenhouse kit will provide the greenhouse hobbyist with an environment to cultivate plants and crops year-round. It's a rewarding hobby that will give you many years of fresh veggies, herbs, fruits, and beautiful plants. The pleasure that it provides is simply indescribable!

Of late, this hobby has become less expensive. This is due to the introduction of modern components that have lowered the cost and increased these structures' overall lifespan.

Benefits of Buying a Greenhouse Kit

A range of benefits are associated with buying ready-to-use greenhouse kits. Some of these advantages include:

- Easy to assemble if instructions are followed.
- Ready to use once assembly has been completed.

- No additional planning time is required since the plans are already provided.
- The added convenience of having the package delivered.
- Buying from a reputable manufacturer will bring peace of mind.
- Most greenhouse kits come with some form of warranty and/or guarantee.
- Some ready-to-use kits come with accessories.
- There's a wide variety to choose from.
- Most manufacturers offer after-sales service.
- Some of the kits can be expanded later if desired.

Disadvantages of Buying a Greenhouse Kit

There really aren't many disadvantages to these products; however, there will be some pre-purchase homework that needs to be done. Buying a greenhouse kit can be a significant decision and should be done following your budget and individual needs. As with any new purchase in unchartered territory, a hobbyist needs to understand the cost of running a greenhouse operation.

Considerations Before Buying a Greenhouse Kit

When building a greenhouse, you must first ensure that the purchased type fits your living environment. If you live in an area frequently covered by snow, you'll need to invest in a robust kit.

Another crucial factor to consider is that greenhouses lose heat during cold temperatures. Therefore, if the plan is to use the greenhouse year-round, it will be important to look at pre-insulated covering materials that promote heat retention.

Conversely, if you live in a very hot area, you would have to invest in additional cooling and ventilation and ensure that there is sufficient shade. For this reason, the greenhouse type and accessories will be very important.

Types of Greenhouse Kits

There are various types of greenhouse kits. Let's take a look at them in more detail.

Cold frames

Even though this is not really a greenhouse, it can be classified as a "small greenhouse." They are great to use as extenders or season starters.

Cool

These applications are also called "frost-free" greenhouses and maintain a stable temperature range between 40–45 degrees fahrenheit. This makes it a perfect choice to serve as a nursery for starter crops and germinating seeds. The best of all? This greenhouse typically doesn't require additional heat and light sources.

Grower

These greenhouses are large and feature adjustable shelves, allowing you to cultivate plants on a long-term basis indoors and under cover of shelter. They come with either opaque or semi-opaque coverings.

This might be ideal if you are looking for an excellent, versatile greenhouse for seeds or indoor crops, with enough space to cure harvests and prep them for storage.

Hothouse

Hot houses have a stable temperature range of 65–70 degrees fahrenheit and higher. Therefore, they are ideally suited for propagating and cultivating exotic plants and tropical vegetation. However, remember that special growing lights and heaters are needed for the plants to grow.

Freestanding

These are also referred to as stand-alone structures. They can be placed anywhere where there is space, permitted that it receives plenty of sunlight, and are erected on level surfaces.

Some kits even have the added benefit of being portable. Many freestanding frames exist, including conventional, geodesic, arch-shaped, and more, as discussed in the previous chapter.

Lean-To

The most significant advantage of lean-to (attached) greenhouses is that you don't require four walls. Instead, you only need one wall that can bear the weight. These structures are also affordable and ideal for small growing applications.

Starter

These kits range in sizes from small to medium and are popular among greenhouse hobbyists for starter plants and seeds transplanted later.

An added advantage is that these structures can double as a potting shed to house all the gardening implements. These applications often come with semi-opaque or transparent coverings to promote direct light for seed propagation.

Warm

This application boasts a uniform temperature range of 50–55 degrees. This makes these kits ideal for growing flowers and vegetables. However, these crops might require additional heat and light sources during winter nighttime seasons.

Available Greenhouse Accessories

The beauty of greenhouse kits is that most of them come with handy accessories in the box. However, there might be some additions that you'd want to add to ensure your greenhouse growing endeavors are successful.

One option is to invest in a starter greenhouse and add some of the recommended extras to it as your budget permits.

Custom Shelving

The possibilities here are endless! Different colors and styles are available for greenhouse shelving, meaning you can completely customize your greenhouse look. They are an excellent solution for extra storage inside your structure.

Louvers (automatic)

Greenhouse kits generally come with vents that can open to control the heat inside the greenhouse. However, you can invest in automatic solar–powered louvers that can do some of the hard work. The louvers will shut and open based on the temperature detected in the air.

Galvanized Steel Braces

This is a great tool to use to reinforce the greenhouse foundation. These steel braces are convenient in areas where the greenhouse will be exposed to strong winds and heavy rain/snowfall.

Greenhouse Shade Cloths

This accessory is perfect for greenhouses with transparent or semi-opaque greenhouses, aiding with temperature cooling inside the structure. These cloths come in various densities, such as UV-stabilized knitted fabrics. There is also a cheaper alternative to using split-bamboo blinds that can be bought from most shops.

These cloths can be installed on the structure's apex, making them easy to draw back if and when needed.

Hand-Watering Wands

Tiny sprouted crops are easily flattened by exposing them to a water spray that is too strong. The addition of hand–watering wands can eliminate this problem and is also crafted to reach the back of the seedling trays on different shelves without breaking your back. The adjustable nozzles also allow uniform misting control, ensuring the soil around the delicate sprouts is not disturbed.

Heaters

There are a plethora of different greenhouse heaters available on the market. Although grow lights aid in plant heat retention, they are not known for heating the soil. Some heat lamps, such as the toaster-coil, can spot corner heat. There are also more complex options, such as the track system attached to the greenhouse ceiling that can spread warmth through the entire greenhouse when required.

Irrigation Systems (automatic)

A greenhouse hobbyist can suffer significant financial loss and heartache when forgetting to water the crops and seedlings. Therefore systems such as mat irrigation, tape irrigation, and other drip-irrigation systems can be installed. The great news is that these automatic systems can be run on battery-operated timers and are relatively inexpensive.

Potting benches

If you plan to grow crops from seeds, you'll need a sturdy work surface. This is where soil benches come into play. A container to house the potting soil can be an effortless way to sweep the spilled earth back into the bag. It's a versatile addition to your greenhouse and can be used as a storage bench, ensuring that your greenhouse is neat and tidy.

Next, let's look at how you can construct a greenhouse, but this time using sustainable waste materials.

Building a Greenhouse From Waste Materials

More great news here as you can also build a greenhouse using waste or recycled materials.

Using some old materials mentioned below, you can set up a sustainable greenhouse in no time.

Old Windows

These preloved structures can be used in various ways to create a simple greenhouse structure. For example, one window can be used to craft a cold-frame structure with the addition of a hinged lid to make a raised bed. This is an ideal coverage solution for a small vegetable patch or even smaller crops that don't take lightly to cold temperatures.

A few windows can also be strung together in various ways to create a mini-greenhouse and can even be attached to an existing house wall to make a small lean-to greenhouse.

Plastic and Other Collateral

You can construct an arch-shaped greenhouse using a sheet of clear tarp and add some metal arches. This is a great way to reduce plastic waste in our ocean and provide excellent protection to your crops.

You can even use an old trampoline by cutting the hoop in the middle and installing a used, transparent tarp over it. An alternative method is using a malleable wood such as cedar by bending it into a hoop shape and then covering it with a type of plastic.

Any leftover wood, plastic, or aluminum can be used to construct a greenhouse, and any old type of door can be used.

You can collect plastic juice and soda bottles to protect smaller plants and seeds if you want something considerably smaller. These materials are excellent at offering protection against pests. All you need to do is remove the bottom part and place it over the plant in the soil. Remove any caps, and you'll have a makeshift opening for airflow. Just ensure that the bottle is wedged deep enough in the soil so insects can't reach the plants and they can't be blown over by the wind.

Used wood pallets

Wood pallets are one of the most versatile recycled materials on the planet. They can be repurposed for a variety of greenhouse uses. Fair enough, taking the individual pallets apart can be a time-consuming task, but it will become easier over time when one has the right tools.

Now that we've covered most of the requirements, let's take a deep dive into the required equipment.

CHAPTER 11:
GREENHOUSE EQUIPMENT

Once your greenhouse is fully set-up, we now need to look at the basic required equipment before adding the crops.

Installing Greenhouse Equipment

There's no denying that greenhouse gardening has many benefits for those eager to learn and invest. The temperature in a greenhouse can be controlled no matter which climate you reside in. No matter if you decide to buy or build one, you are definitely going to need a few supplies to get started.

Installing your greenhouse is only the departure point of your growing adventures. There are many factors to consider, such as humidity, lighting, sanitation, temperature, watering, and even the types of plants to grow.

Below, I've set out my general go-to greenhouse supply list. For ease of reference, I've broken the different types down.

Basic Equipment

Some of the basic items a greenhouse gardener will require include items such as:

- a variety of different pots
- containers to house various growing mediums
- a selection of hand trowels
- seedling trays and flats

Benches

Both shelves and benches can be used. The only thing really required is something that will house your plants off the ground. Wood surfaces can be painted with a semi-gloss glazing paint. This makes cleaning a breeze and protects wooden shelves and benches from mold.

Climate Control

An evaporative cooler or heater will be needed if you plan to use the greenhouse application for the whole year. Greenhouse heaters are a cheap and great addition to small structures, and fans can be used to cool structures in milder climates and to move hot air out of the application. In addition, hygrometers and thermometers featuring climate control systems can be used for accurate control.

Drainage and Irrigation

Your crops will require water. Large and commercially-sized greenhouse operations will typically use drip-irrigation systems to water crops. However, smaller greenhouse structures can be watered by hand. Don't water plants with a hose-sprayer since this can disturb the soil around the plants and could also increase the risk of spreading mold spores.

Drainage is also a crucial factor. Increased drainage can be achieved by slanting the benches slightly to prevent water pooling. There's also the option to drill holes into the benches to allow the droplets to seep through and possibly water plants beneath that require less moisture.

Lighting

Most greenhouse applications will require some type of artificial lighting to ensure the plants are adequately lit inside. This is where the addition of fluorescent lights comes into play. However, remember that this might be a cost-prohibitive juncture for small greenhouse operations.

Sanitation

Proper sanitation is another crucial factor to consider. The last thing you'd want is bacteria and pets to enter your greenhouse and destroy all your hard work. So invest in the appropriate chemicals to keep your application clean and disease-free.

Shade

If some of your crops are exposed to too much sunlight, you must invest in shade cloths to keep the harmful sun rays at bay during the hot summer months.

Ventilation

Adding one or two additional vents to your greenhouse will help regulate the humidity level and release pent-up heat. Your crops will thrive when you can maintain a good ventilation level.

Part One Summary: Greenhouse Investment vs. Cost

We've reached the end of the first part of the book. I'd like to conclude by showing you how you can save money on groceries by growing your own wholesome fruits, veggies, and herbs.

Saving Money on Groceries

According to a study by the National Gardening Association (NGA), a small garden could save you a lot of money on groceries. The study concluded that an average–sized greenhouse could produce around 300 pounds of fresh crops, totaling a whopping $600. This calculation was based on the premise that an average greenhouse hobbyist invests between $70 and $530 (National Gardening Association, n.d.).

Another case study detailed that one participant enjoyed excellent yields and cost–saving measures from their greenhouse. The participant maintained various summer gardens ranging in size from 12 x 14 feet and 33 x 3 feet. They had an initial startup cost of $278 with the introduction of livestock heating inside the applications. Altogether, had they purchased the same crop yields at a local store, the bill would've totaled $1,770.89, meaning she enjoyed savings of no less than $1,492.89. (Piper, 2020)

What a great saving initiative! Let's look at some top tips and tricks to achieve this.

Only Plant What you Eat

The first step here is exactly as the previous line suggests. Look at your grocery list, and then plan the crops to grow. Only plant the herbs, fruits, and vegetables that you actually use in the kitchen and those consumed regularly.

Grow Crops From Seeds

You can start cultivating plants indoors in the late spring, permitting you have the required space and some time on your hands. Seeds are a great way to go about this. You'll always get more yields than intended. This gives you a great platform to get some friends and family involved and trade seeds or enjoy the crops together by splitting the initial costs.

A typical example includes tomatoes. Vine tomatoes can rake up to $2.29 per pound. A six-punnet of tomatoes yields between 15 to 25 pounds per plant at the store. To put it into perspective, a pack of seeds costs even less. Typically there are about 20 seeds inside a tomato seed packet, and each tomato plant can produce between 10 to 30 pounds of fresh tomatoes. An average pack of tomato seeds generally costs about $3.21. You do the math!

Maximize your yield

The best is that you don't need a big greenhouse or garden to start enjoying the benefits of your own crops. You can begin with crops that produce high-yields, such as leaf lettuce, onions, and tomatoes.

Most newbie greenhouse gardeners make the mistake of not adequately using vertical greenhouse space. Many different types of plants can be cultivated and grown in hangers and eventually become climbing plants that grow against the walls. This means that the horizontal space is still at your disposal.

However, to deploy this method, some planning will be required. A handy tip might be to keep tabs on when you plant crops, what was planted, and the harvest. This will help you choose the plants to grow next year.

Plan and plant ahead to eat later

It's always advisable to plan and grow more crops than intended. Yes, sure, you can eat fresh, wholesome foods, but the surplus can also be used in other ways, such as chopping them up and freezing them, and transforming them into other products such as jellies and preserves.

Some crops like carrots, onions, potatoes, pumpkins, and certain winter squashes can be stored for a long time without needing much processing.

There's also the option of planting, keeping the winter months in mind. If you can extend the growing season, making your produce last, you'll have fresh crops through the year and well into the winter before the planting season commences again.

It's much more than just food!

Even just on a small scale, gardening has the power to provide food to impoverished communities. Not only can it create jobs, but it serves as a means for the people to grow their own sustainable food right in their backyard.

Other far-reaching benefits include spending time with the family outdoors and teaching children the value of growing their own food. And this is on top of all the cost-saving measures as well.

A little Help!

I hope you have enjoyed the first part of Greenhouse Gardening and have learned some valuable tips for starting your own greenhouse projects. I have tried to make the format beginner-friendly while balancing general information and details for getting started.

Please consider writing a favorable review on **Amazon** if you have found the ideas helpful. I have put a lot of effort into writing it and I am pleased to share my knowledge with you.

PART TWO:
HOW TO GROW PLANTS

CHAPTER 12:
GROWING GREENHOUSE VEGETABLES, HERBS, FRUITS, AND FLOWERS

Finally, we've reached the good part of the book, where you are now ready to start exploring what it takes to cultivate the different types of crops.

The subchapters listed in this chapter will be dedicated to describing in detail the process and steps to take to grow flowers, fruits, herbs, and vegetables in a greenhouse application. But, first things first, let's explore how a greenhouse can help extend a growing season.

Season-Extending Techniques

Few greenhouse gardeners will be satisfied with the length of the growing season. For example, those living in the northern parts of the globe will barely have sufficient time to harvest ripe melons and tomatoes. Similarly, those living in the southern parts experience scorching heat and droughts, limiting their growing activities. This means that typically they only have the fall and spring months at their disposal for growing plants.

However, deploying a few straightforward strategies to extend the season and protect the plants can mean the difference between a short and an extended growing season. With the techniques below, you can extend the growing season to two-six months (and beyond).

Limit wind exposure

If you live in an area riddled with strong winds, your plants need extra energy to withstand the elements. So instead of focusing on root growth, they deploy their energy merely to survive.

You can protect your garden by erecting a wooden fence, putting up netting for windbreaks, or even planting shrubs and trees that serve as a windbreak. The key is limiting the wind speed but not ultimately killing it.

In the case of a prevailing wind direction, it might only be necessary to build a fence on that specific side. However, if this is not the case and financial constraints are in play, you could use a temporary plastic mesh fence or cold frames and other structures created with fabrics. You'd find that seedlings cultivated under garden fabric might produce twice as many yields.

Heat the soil

Extra heat can be provided to the plants in winter by covering the plants with a layer of mulch. However, remember to remove the mulch at the start of spring to allow the sunlight to reach the soil.

Another method is creating raised beds or covering the cold soil with black plastic. Black plastic can boost soil temperature by several degrees, and it can also be left on the whole season and removed before transplanting. The combination of black plastic or mulch will kick start crops like melons and others that prefer warm soil to grow.

During the fall season, the garden fabric can provide the required heat to the same heat-loving plant types.

Heat and Sun Protection

Controlling hot weather can be just as tricky as managing cold weather. Luckily shade nets are specially developed to keep both soil and plants cool and retain water.

Block Fall and Spring Frost

Frost is a limiting factor and significant concern for most gardeners due to the fall and spring seasons. It requires only one cold night to kill even the most robust plants. In emergencies, items such as cut-up boxes, blankets, and sheets can be used. However, with the advancement of greenhouse fabrics for precisely this purpose, this task has now been made easier. Garden fabric covers can withstand temperatures 25 degrees and lower.

Alternatively, portable greenhouses and cold frame structures provide increased protection against the cold, enabling you to extend your harvest and growing seasons through the winter.

Three Ways to Stretch Your Harvest

The first step here is to consider your local climate. Next, you need to ask yourself how far you want to stretch your growing season and how much time you have on your hands?

If you reside in a cold climate and want to stretch the harvesting season throughout the year, you will need to purchase a greenhouse application, but be warned this will require daily devotion and care.

Alternatively, if you are only seeking a few additional weeks, there are three types of techniques at your disposal (plus they're cost-efficient too):

30 Days Extended Growing

You can give your seedlings a much-needed boost by providing them with a sheltered growing area. Then, when the time comes to transplant them, try to keep them covered with a piece of garden fabric for the first few weeks. In this instance, it's advisable to use a garden fabric crafted from polypropylene or polyester to ensure that extra heat can escape and moisture can trickle through. After that, the only other monitoring required will be to check the crops weekly, ensure they're watered, and tend to weeds.

Alternatively, recycled plastic ware and bottles can cover tiny sprouts. Ensure that the plants receive adequate ventilation and look out for overheating signs.

60 Days Extended Growing

The garden fabric method can be used here as well. Use the fabric in fall and spring, and enjoy the benefits of a two-month extended harvest season. A lighter material will be used during spring, but the fall season will require a more robust fabric to keep the heat inside.

The crops you choose to grow will also considerably impact the ability to extend a harvest season since certain plants are better suited to late or early season production. For example, certain types of broccoli prefer to grow in cool spring soil but can seed almost instantly when the ground is heated.

90-120 Days Extended Growing

You might think that extending a growing season is hard, but it's relatively easy. One of the best tips I can share is to focus on a few crops at a time and not attempt to extend the harvest seasons right away for all the plants you are trying to grow simultaneously. The growth seasons of root vegetables and salad greens are the easiest to extend (permitting you follow a strict schedule).

Chapter 13: Greenhouse Pollination

Before we enter into the part relating to the growing plants, here are some basic concepts regarding the definition of pollination and how it can be generated in a greenhouse.

What is pollination?

Pollination can be categorized as the method of depositing grains of pollen from the male (anther) of a flower to the (stigma) female. Plants can be either:

- **Cross-pollinated**: This is where it needs a vector, such as wind, to transfer the pollen between flowers.
- **Self-pollinated**: Where the plant can fertilize itself.

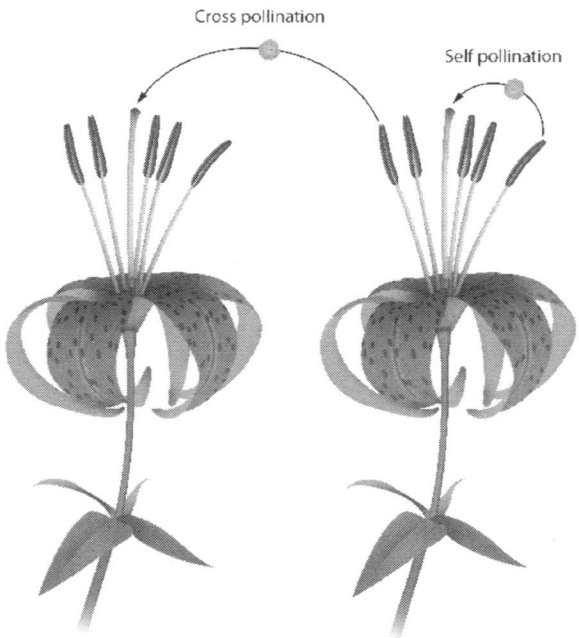

How does pollination occur in nature?

The different flower traits of various pollinators are called pollination syndromes. Plants that flower have evolved in nature utilizing two methods:

- **Abiotic**: Meaning that the plant can develop without organisms.
- **Biotic**: Meaning pollination is mediated by animals such as bees.

It's estimated that around 80% of plant pollination is biotically facilitated, and 20% is abiotically pollinated (consisting of 2% water and 98% by species).

Examples of greenhouse plants that require pollination

- apples
- barley
- currants
- eggplant
- grapes
- mulberries
- okra
- peaches
- sour cherries
- tomatoes

Examples of greenhouse plants that don't require pollination

- basil
- cabbage
- garlic
- kohlrabi
- leafy greens
- onion
- potatoes
- rosemary
- sweet potatoes
- turmeric
- yams

Three Types of Greenhouse Pollination

Bee pollination

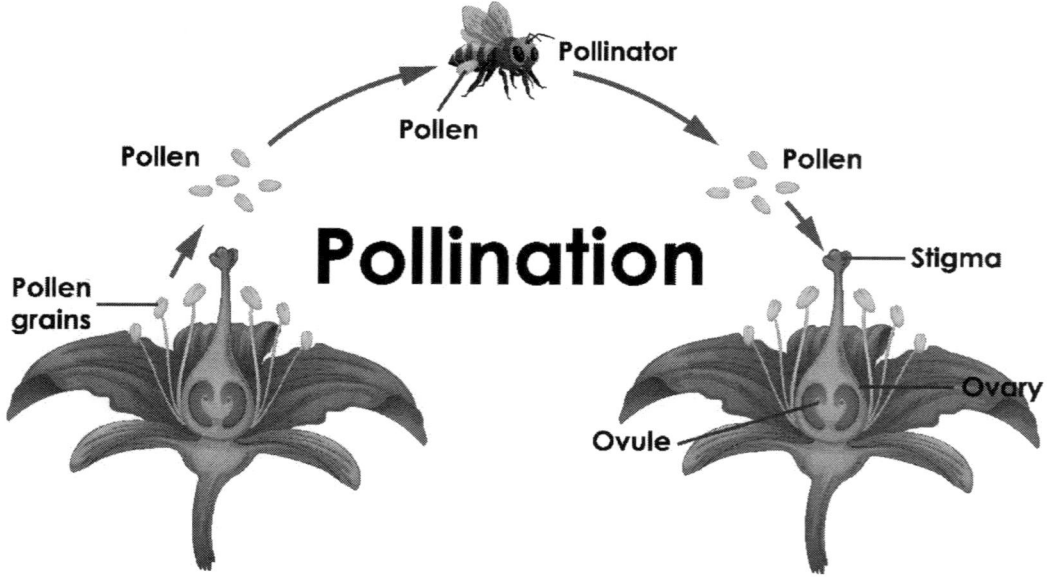

As a bee collects pollen and nectar from a plant's flower, some of the pollen grains of the stamen (male reproductive organ on a flower) stick to the hair of the bee's body. When the bee collects nectar from a secondary flower, these grains are deposited in the pistil or stigma (the female flower's reproductive organ). This then promotes pollination, whereby seeds and flowers can develop.

Pros

- Reduced labor cost.
- Increased return on investment (ROI)

The most significant benefit of using bees in greenhouses is their ability to reduce the cost of labor. There's no need for manual pollination as the bees will do all the hard work for you. This then results in lower consumer prices on a commercial scale.

Furthermore, with bees in a greenhouse, you promote adding essential vitamins and minerals to food crops.

Cons

- Risk of bee stings, including allergic reaction
- Potential disease or parasite spread by traveling bees

One drawback of having bees around is the risk of getting stung. Not only does it hurt, but it's a potential health hazard for those with allergies-especially if it comes to you and your workforce. However, the benefits far outweigh the disadvantages since bees mainly sting when provoked or when they see a territorial threat.

Secondly, our bee populations have contributed to spreading diseases and parasites recently.

Device pollination

This is also referred to as artificial pollination and is a method that requires human intervention. It's a technique used to pollinate crops without undesirable and insufficient natural pollination. It doesn't require the aid of weather or insects.

Pros

Artificially pollinating crops is useful in using one plant's genetics with another and creating a more specific plant adaptation.

Cons

Two disadvantages of artificial pollination are that fertilization is not guaranteed, and the process is time-consuming. In addition, research related to artificial pollination takes time (especially for staff training). If the method is not done correctly, the flower could wilt and die without yielding any desired results.

Manual pollination

This is also referred to as hand pollination. This technique is facilitated by manually depositing pollen from one plant's male part to another female plant's pistil.

Pros

One of the biggest advantages of hand pollination is that it produces plant yields without natural pollinators.

Cons

One drawback of hand pollination is the time needed to manually pollinate plants, especially if you have many that require pollination to grow.

Without further adieu, let's get started on seed cultivation.

CHAPTER 14:
SEED STARTING

We kick our greenhouse gardening endeavors off with seed starting. Therefore, the first subtopic to cover is seed propagation and its respective requirements.

Asexual vs. Sexual Propagation

First, let's take a look at each in more detail.

Asexual propagation (also called vegetative propagation) entails taking a piece of a parent plant and then cultivating it to grow itself into a new version of itself. The result is a unique plant genetically identical to the parent crop. The leaves, roots, or stems are typically used in this process.

Pros

Some benefits attached to asexual seed propagation include:

- It's quicker and cheaper than other techniques.
- Ability to obtain new varieties.
- Establishment of hybrid vigor.
- It's a viable means for seed propagation.
- Decreased risk of disease transmission.
- All plants cloned are identical to their parents.
- Suitable propagating solution for plants that are hard to cultivate.

Cons

Some of the drawbacks associated with asexual propagation are:

- It's labor-intensive.
- Except in the case of tissue culture, this method entails that only a few plants can be propagated from the parent.

Using Asexual Propagation

Most greenhouse plants are propagated using the asexual method. Some crops that thrive with this process are woody ornamental and herbaceous plants, cranberries, cassava, potatoes, sweet potatoes, strawberries, and cane fruit.

Sexual propagation is when the egg and pollen form a union. It then uses the genes of two parent plants to create a third. This process sprouts typically from the floral sections of a plant.

<u>Pros</u>

Some advantages associated with sexual seed propagation include:

- Produces high-crop yields in a short amount of time.
- Produces hybrids.
- The process can handle large numbers at a time.

<u>Cons</u>

Conversely, there are also some disadvantages associated with sexual propagation. These include:

- Certain plants are not producing viable seeds.
- Some seeds might be slow to germinate or might germinate with incredible difficulty.
- Some generic viability can occur due to the formation of hybrids.

Using Sexual Propagation

The sexual propagation process can be used for plants such as lettuce, okra, muskmelons, nicotiana, and eggplants.

CHAPTER 15:
GROWING MEDIUMS FOR SEED STARTING

The best soil for seed starting is a mix of compost, potting mix, and loam soil. You can prepare this combination using 60% loam and 30% compost; the remaining 10% is made of potting mix. The potting mixture consists of materials such as vermiculite, peat moss, and perlite.

If your native soil is of poor quality, you can add half compost and half potting mix. However, be aware that the percentage of peat moss content should not exceed 20%. This is because the soil is naturally acidic and can damage vegetable crops.

pH Level

Each plant species has a preferred pH soil range for growing. However, most plants prefer a soil pH range between 5.4 and 6.8.

Soil Temperature

The general rule of thumb for an optimal soil temperature inside a greenhouse is between 70-80 degrees for all plants.

Moisture level

In the case of greenhouse applications,, the ideal humidity level should range between 40-80%.

The Different Types of Containers for Seed Starting

Selecting suitable pots and containers for seed starting can be a complex task since there is no one perfect solution. Your choice of containers and pots will depend on many factors, such as:

- quality of the plants
- size of the crops
- budget vs. required upfront costs
- renewability

For this reason, there are several options to select in this regard. Some include:

Air Pots

This type of container has been designed with the concept of root air pruning. The containers are built in such a manner to guide plant roots through a tunnel that has been cut open to allow airflow. Once the tips of the roots reach this opening, they are dried out by the air. The tip then terminates and creates more roots from the crops.

Using regular containers will yield a round ball of tangled roots. The bigger the crop grows, the bigger the ball will get. This is because crops that aren't watered properly will send extra roots to the already big root ball. Crops grown in these pots have a fibrous and dense network of what is referred to as feeder roots, meaning there is no entanglement involved either. It's one of the only genuine air pruning systems that can achieve this effect.

Air pots are ideally suited for growing trees and herbs. These plants are also referred to as perennials and are usually permanent garden fixtures.

These potting systems are more expensive compared to other solutions. Therefore it's advisable to use this seed–starting solution for larger sprouts and seedlings that need more time to mature before being transplanted outdoors.

Rating Metrics

Plant quality: 2/5

Startup cost: 0/5

Plant size: 5/5

Reusability: 5/5

Cell Packs and Trays

Cell packs (also called seedling trays) boast small soil cells for each plant. This highly dense system permits many different plants to be housed in a small space. Each cell is placed in a tray that provides a secure structure during transportation. These trays also store excess water and ensure that everything is kept neat.

These types of systems are prevalent and inexpensive to use. The added benefit is that they only need a tiny bit of soil dedicated to each seed. These systems are ideal for small-scale greenhouse applications.

However, they do have some drawbacks. The flats can prove challenging to water. Top irrigation is ideal for this purpose, but it can become quite messy if you have a small greenhouse structure inside your house. It's advisable to rather water this potting system from the bottom to avoid unwanted spillages. Another disadvantage is that this system is easily overwatered-the cells can become too moist, and the seedlings located at the ends can dry out quicker, making them susceptible to plant diseases. Most of the issues can be mitigated by using a wicking mat that self–waters.

Rating Metrics

Plant quality: 5/5

Startup cost: 4/5

Plant size: 2/5

Reusability: 2/5

Cone-Tainers

This method was initially developed for the forestry industry to propagate juvenile tree seedlings. These containers are deep and perfectly suited to crops with a long taproot. They are also narrow, meaning they can be used for high-plant density crops.

Cone-tainers are perfect for home greenhouse applications, but there are a few factors to consider. One drawback is the limited available space and the fact that they are not easy to find at gardening outlets. This means they are commonly available to purchase online but at a higher cost than other container options.

Furthermore, the cone-tainers will need a stand to house them. Therefore, this might not be a viable container option if you are looking at using it in batches. This makes it quite cumbersome to move plants around and not really be able to water them from below. Cone-tainers are best used for growing vertical crops such as leeks and onions from seeds due to the nature of the plants.

Rating Metrics

Plant quality: 5/5

Startup cost: 2/5

Plant size: 3/5

Reusability: 4/5

Jiffy pellets

Jiffy pellets are little compact discs made from coir or peat moss. When watered, they expand after a while. This is an excellent option for beginner greenhouse hobbyists since each disc serves as a pot on its own, with all the required nutrients and potting mix a tiny seed would need to grow.

This potting system is also ideally suited to the air prune method for the side roots. However, some gardeners have experienced challenges using this method since the netting must be cut away once transplant time comes to allow the plants to grow fully.

Three significant benefits of this potting system are that the pellets come in various sizes, meaning it's a suitable solution for different crop sizes. Secondly, jiffy pellets are easy to find at an affordable price from most gardening retailers. Lastly, you don't have to purchase additional seed starting mix because it already has the required potting mix per se.

Rating Metrics

Plant quality: 5/5

Startup cost: 4/5

Plant size: 3/5

Reusability: 1/5

Net cups

Net cups were specially designed for hydroponics applications. It's a basked–shaped cut featuring open slits at the bottom and sides. These slits promote the unrestrained growth of plant roots in high-humidity or nutrient-rich solutions.

This is another example of the air pruning method; the cups are placed on a watering mat that permits them to draw moisture if and when needed. Again, net cups can be purchased in bulk at an affordable price.

The smaller cups are cheap but can be flimsy. On the other hand, the larger cups can support bigger sprouts and are easier to reuse than their smaller counterparts.

Plant quality: 4/5

Startup cost: 4/5

Plant size: 3/5

Reusability: 3/5

Old cups and food containers

This is probably the most renewable and cost-effective option out of all. If you are tight on budget, you can simply wash out used cups and food containers and be ready to go with your first seedlings. The only other thing to do would be cut holes at the bottom for drainage purposes.

The great thing about this container system is that the put doesn't have to be filled with potting mix to the brim, especially if you plant crops that don't feature aggressive route systems, and the soil can be reused. Plants like tomatoes can be transplanted before they produce roots and become too big for the pot.

Rating Metrics

Plant quality: 3/5

Startup cost: 5/5

Plant size: 4/5

Reusability: 5/5

Peat pots

These containers are easily recognizable by their resemblance to cardboard pulp. This is an environmentally-friendly option since most peat pots are made from biodegradable materials. You will plant the seeds in these containers and simply stick them into the soil, whereby the pot will decompose, and the plant will mature in size.

One challenge in using this method is that sometimes the pot doesn't break down, which stunts plant growth. This can be avoided by peeling away the pot and tossing it into the soil during the transplantation process to aid decomposition.

Rating Metrics

Plant quality: 4/5

Startup cost: 4/5

Plant size: 4/5

Reusability: 1/5

Salvaged pots

Salvaged pots refer to any pots and containers you've purchased for other plants. Trust me, these are very handy, especially if you plan on gifting a friend with a potted plant.

It's a no-brainer that this method makes a lot of sense. Not only does it save you money, but it also encourages recycling.

Rating Metrics

Plant quality: 3/5

Startup cost: 5/5

Plant size: 5/5

Reusability: 5/5

Seedling pots

This is a straightforward and reliable way to grow seeds. You simply need to select the shape and size required for each plant. Personally, I've found that the 2.25 inch square-shaped containers provide the perfect balance for most plant roots in a limited space.

This potting system permits a greenhouse gardener to scale bigger or smaller in terms of crop quantity. In addition, the containers can easily be moved around to increase airflow. Another great benefit is that the pots can be reused, and the crops can be watered from the bottom or placed onto a self-watering mat.

One drawback is that it can get hard to manage many different-sized pots.

Rating Metrics

Plant quality: 4/5

Startup cost: 4/5

Plant size: 4/5

Reusability: 5/5

Soil blockers

Soil blockers are an ingenious invention. They are made of a soil mix and come in cubes or blocks to grow seeds in. Each individual blocker can be pressed out to form multiple blocks. They are similar to ice cube trays in that a miniature air space separates each blocker. Each series of blockers can be placed on a tray.

One great benefit of this potting system is starting with a large volume of small, medium, and large seedlings. As the crops mature, soil blockers can be upgraded by fitting the smaller blocks into bigger blocks. The best way to water this system is to supply water at the bottom by placing the blockers on a capillary mat.

One consideration is that this system's upfront cost is expensive. However, no waste is involved, meaning it's long-term sustainable. On the other hand, I've found one significant disadvantage in using this system: if you have physical limitations, it might be challenging to manage so many containers simultaneously.

Rating Metrics

Plant quality: 5/5

Startup cost: 2/5

Plant size: 3/5

Reusability: 5/5

Planting Greenhouse Seeds

Planting seeds is pretty straightforward. You only need to fill each tray with two to three seeds and fill the container with a seed-raising mix. The next step is to wipe off extra soil gently and remember not to compact the potting/soil mix. Lastly, gently mist each seed tray and place it on the appropriate bench or shelf in your greenhouse, based on its individual light and shade requirements.

Fertilizing Seeds

Do I need to fertilize my seedlings? In short, yes! Although seeds boast sufficient power to germinate by themselves, they still require essential nutrients for optimum growth not typically found in the soil. In addition, it's known that young seedlings battling to grow lack the proper growth-nutrients.

Phosphorus and nitrogen are two essential nutrients in seed starting fertilization. It's the two most commonly found fertilizers that promote crop growth. It's essential not to fertilize your seeds before they've sprouted. Once the first sprouts have emerged, you mist them with a water–soluble fertilizer at ¼ standard strength. This should be done once bi-weekly, slowly increasing the fertilizer concentration as your young seedlings produce more leaves.

But be aware that too much fertilizer can be just as harmful as not providing enough! Ensure that the guidelines on the brand label are followed and don't permit granular fertilizer to touch the plant directly, which might cause burns.

Watering Seeds

The best watering system for seeds is a misting system that can connect to the main house and be operated when needed. You can also join the misting system to a tap timer that will provide an automated misting solution.

The length of time to water is plant and location dependent. However, the soil needs to be consistently moist to ensure healthy seedlings. The best tip I can give here is to check the seed trays after each watering and adjust the schedule as needed.

Growing Vegetables in a Greenhouse

There's no denying that with so many options, deciding what actually to grow can be an overwhelming choice. And with growing veggies in a greenhouse, there are also temperature concerns for each season.

My best piece of advice here is to select vegetables that love to grow indoors and the ones you plan on selling or eating regularly. Vegetables such as peppers, lettuce, other leafy greens, peas, beans, and cucumbers are most commonly consumed. Furthermore, consider growing greens that can tolerate cold weather and vegetables such as peppers that can withstand the heat the best in summer.

The type of veggies you will cultivate will largely depend on three factors, namely:

- your zone
- the temperature inside your greenhouse
- the amount of space you have to grow them

Remember also to have fun experimenting with growing weird and wonderful crops, apart from the tried-and-tested stalwarts like onions and tomatoes.

Why grow vegetables in a greenhouse

Greenhouse applications and similar indoor growing places are great for first–time greenies. Imagine getting to a place where you can enjoy your own homegrown veggies without worrying about the climate outside or being limited to seasonal vegetables and crops. The good news is that growing plants indoors opens the door to all sorts of possibilities!

Investing in a greenhouse implies that your crops will be protected against harsh elements they'd otherwise typically face outdoors, such as winds, heat, snow, and rain. In addition, with greenhouse growing now at your fingertips, you can now create the optimal conditions for your crops to grow to the best of their ability. The reason behind it is that you have control over components such as:

- fertilization
- humidity
- irrigation
- light
- moisture
- temperature

Which are the best vegetables to grow in a greenhouse?

As you embark on the journey of deciding which veggies to plant in your greenhouse, it might be good to do some homework on the ones that thrive in a controlled environment. With this in mind, you might choose between warm or cold seasoned veggies or the ones that prefer a specific type of climate (such as more heat).

Heat-loving plants that yield high gains and grow well include jalapenos, chilies, tomatoes, okra, and sweet bell peppers. Should you prefer to invest in veggies that love the sun but prefer moderate to low temperatures at night, your best options would be crops like cantaloupe, eggplant, and summer squash.

Conversely, if you're considering going with veggies that prefer a colder climate, some options include peas, chard, and beets.

Let's take a deep-dive into some vegetables to grow in your greenhouse.

Chapter 16:
Three Vegetables to Grow in a Greenhouse

Below we will discuss the cultivation of three different vegetables inside a greenhouse application.

Tiara Cabbage

Scientific Name: *Brassica oleracea*

Description

This is a highly nutritious and diverse staple vegetable. Cabbage is often categorized similarly to other vegetables such as lettuce and kale due to its appearance. But, in actual fact, its true classification is that of a cruciferous vegetable.

Plant uses

Plant uses will depend on the variety of cabbage. Some types include green, red, savoy, napa, bok choy, and brussels sprouts. Some food items you can make from cabbage are stir-fries, sauerkraut, and coleslaw.

How to grow Tiara cabbage

For this specific purpose, we will use the Tiara cabbage variant

Humidity

Cabbage needs a relative humidity level ranging between 90–95%.

Temperature

Cabbage is versatile and can be grown in early spring, fall, and winter.

Early spring

Using the midseason and early varieties, sow two seeds per cell in 50–72 cell plug flat trays, with three to four seeds each. So for one packet of seeds, you'll yield about 20 rows of flats. If you plan on planting them in outdoor beds, the seeds need to be about ¼ inches embedded in the soil.

During this phase, the ideal growth temperature should be over 75°F until the seeds have germinated. Once germination has occurred, decrease the air temperature to 60°F.

The cruciferous plant family thrives in cooler temperatures that range between 55–75°F. The optimum preferred temperature ranges between 60–70°F. It's also known that cabbages produce high yields in warmer, summery climates.

Fall

For this purpose, midseason and storage cabbage varieties should be used. Seeds should start in May and be ready for transplantation between June and July. To secure matured cabbage heads, ensure that the seeds are cropped early in areas before cold temperatures set in.

Winter

Cabbage crops can be grown during winter when the region enjoys moderate temperatures (not below 32°F). Cabbages will be ready for transplantation set out between September and February.

Direct seeding requirements

Plant between three to four seeds 12 inches apart, ½ inch deep, and in rows of 24–36 inches by thinning one plant in each group.

Splitting seeds

Some early cabbage varieties may burst or split when they reach maturity or may be exposed to rapid growth spurts due to heavy irrigation or rainfall that follows directly after a dry season.

Splitting can be somewhat avoided by slowing down the crop's growth. In addition, severing some of its root systems and cultivating it close to the actual plant or twisting the plant slightly include ways to mitigate splitting.

Lighting

Cabbage needs full sun.

Water

Cabbage prefers moist soil. Seeds should be sowed, and an adequate water supply is needed until the crops start germinating. Be aware of soggy soil as this can cause seed splitting, but apply approximately 1.5 inches of water to ensure heads mature.

Soil pH

Cabbage needs fertile soils ranging in pH level between 6.5–7.5. They are heavy feeders that require irrigation consistently during their growing phase.

Transplanting

Cabbage is ready to transplant outdoors between four to six weeks after sowing. First, plant the sprouts between 12–18 inches apart in rows between 18–36 inches apart.

Storage and harvesting

While the heads are still actively growing and green, the best storage temperature is 32°F with a relative humidity level ranging between 95–98%, boasting adequate air circulation. Take care to only store cabbage heads that are free from diseases.

Cabbage is matured and ready for harvesting when 10-14 days are subtracted from warmer temperatures and then adding 14 days after direct seeding has transpired.

Potential pests and diseases

A strict preventative regime is needed to protect the seeds from diseases. This includes rotating long crops with non-brassica crops, cleaning the outdoor seedbeds and starting mixes, and deploying the appropriate sanitation processes. This will protect the crops from diseases such as Black Leg and Black Rot.

Cabbages are prone to potential pests such as root maggots and flea beetles. This issue can be mitigated by covering the crops with row covers, starting from the planting day. Furthermore, insecticides containing *azadirachtin* and *pyrethrin* can be used to help keep critters at bay.

Containers

Cabbages can be planted in containers between 10–12 inches wide and in pretty deep pots. Once ready for transplantation in bigger pots, ensure only one sprout is placed per container. Otherwise, this will result in smaller cabbage heads. If you wish to plant more cabbages in one pot, use a wider container. Ensure that the pot features adequate drainage.

Fertilizer

A once-monthly dosage of a balanced liquid organic fertilizer is sufficient for growing mature cabbage heads. Alternatives include using a 10–5–5 fertilizer or diluted fish emulsion every second week. You can also use compost tea to increase the soil's nutrient levels.

Crispino Lettuce

Scientific Name: *Lactuca sativa*

Description

Lettuce is a leafy vegetable and forms part of the daisy family (*Asteraceae*). It's mostly grown as a leafy vegetable but can be used for seeds and stems in some instances.

Plant uses

Lettuce is predominantly used in salads but can be used in sandwiches, soups, wraps, and can be grilled.

How to grow Crispino lettuce

For this specific example, we will discuss the Crispino lettuce variant.

Humidity

Lettuce prefers a humidity level between 50–70%.

Temperature

Lettuce is a robust crop that prefers cooler weather. It grows best in temperatures ranging between 60–65°F. Lettuce germinates at its best in temperatures below 70°F. Seeds should be sown every two to three weeks to ensure full heads or salad mix.

Direct seeding requirements

Lettuce seeds tend to germinate in soils with an ideal temperature range of 40°F. Four to six seeds should be sown in one-inch rows at least two inches apart. Seeds should only be covered to ⅛ inches and gently firmed into the soil.

Lighting

Lettuce requires at least six hours of broad daylight daily in a south-facing spot.

Water

The dry soil needs to be watered to ensure the coolness of the soil and the required moisture needed to produce uniform germination. Because lettuce prefers a shallow container, you might have to water the crops regularly to prevent them from drying out. Therefore, it's crucial to constantly keep the soil somewhat moist but not overwater them.

Soil pH

Lettuce requires a soil pH of 5.8 to mature to heads.

Transplanting

When the plants are between two and three inches tall, they are ready to be transplanted. Lettuce plants should be hardened off between seven and ten days before transplantation. Hardening lettuce entails placing the containers outside for a few hours per day, slowly increasing daily time.

Storage and harvesting

Head lettuce should be cut at the base, and the wrapper leaves should be kept for handling loss. Cut alternating plants to extend your harvest window. Heads should be packed in layers with the ends cut away, sap washed off and cooled immediately.

For baby leaf lettuce, cut about one inch above its growth point. Any debris should be removed to promote regrowth quality for the remainder of the plant.

It's vital to keep lettuce stored between 35–40°F, away from standing water but in high humidity. Head lettuce can be saved for 14–20 days.

Potential pests and diseases

The pests that lettuce crops are most susceptible to are Thrips and Aphids.

Regarding diseases, lettuce is predisposed to conditions such as anthracnose, black root rot, botrytis, downy mildew, bacterial spots, necrotic yellows, Rhizoctonia, rust sclerotinia rot, soft rot, and spotted wilt.

Containers

The good news is that almost all the lettuce varieties can be cultivated in containers or pots. The plants don't require deep soil and thrive in shallow-wide pots. The containers should feature adequate drainage, should be between six and eight inches deep and can be crafted from any materials.

Fertilizer

When the lettuce seedlings are between three and five inches long, you can apply a 10–10–10 balanced liquid fertilizer to boost growth. You can also incorporate fruit scraps to keep the plants healthy. Once the plants are taller, the feed can be applied every three to four weeks.

Sungold Tomatoes

Scientific Name: *Solanum lycopersicum*

Description

There are over 100 different types of tomatoes for each class. Some types include Roma, plum, paste, grape, cherry, and beefsteak. Tomatoes also come in a variety of colors, sizes, and shapes.

Plant uses

Apart from being used for jams, salads, and as a base ingredient for many dishes, tomatoes also have a lot of nutritional benefits. Although no scientific evidence supports these claims, tomatoes have been known to combat diseases such as cancer and cardiac diseases.

How to grow Sungold tomatoes

Determinate vs. indeterminate tomatoes

Determinate tomatoes grow in a bush, and indeterminate tomatoes grow on vines (climbers).

The determinate varieties don't need to be trimmed and can be cultivated with or without supports, with the fruits ripening in a concentrated period.

The indeterminate tomato varieties should be pruned, caged, or supported for the desired results and take longer to ripen than their determinate counterparts.

Humidity

During the day, tomatoes require a humidity level between 65–75%, and during the night, they need a humidity level ranging between 80–90%

Temperature

During lower nighttime temperatures, auxiliary lights can be used to grow tomatoes. During the early crop yields, plants should be planted under row covers at the time of the last frost date. Great care should be taken not to expose unprotected crops to continual nighttime temperatures below 45°F. Plant tomatoes in rows between four and six inches apart. Tomatoes should be planted deeply to accommodate adventitious rooting.

Determinate tomato varieties should be planted in rows between 12–24 inches apart, and interminates should be planted in rows between 24–34 inches apart.

Pruning and trellising

When it comes to pruning, the indeterminate tomato varieties will primarily benefit when all the suckers from the first branch, below the first flower cluster, are removed. It's known that the suckers on the lower part miss growing on the trellis, sap the energy from the top suckers, and aid in proliferating plant diseases contracted from the soil. Should the lower suckers be needed later, the leaves can be thinned out to promote airflow.

For trellising, perform the basketweave action on every second or third plant. This can be done by pounding the stakes when they are between five and six inches in length. For taller indeterminates, prune the tomato plants once the size becomes unmanageable for easy harvesting.

Lighting

Tomatoes require at least six hours of daily sunlight. However, consider exposing them to up to eight hours of sunlight per day for the best results.

Water

The general rule is that tomatoes need 0.26 gallons of water daily in sunny and hot conditions and less for cooler temperatures.

Soil pH

The optimum soil pH level for tomatoes is between 5.5–7.5.

Transplanting

It's important not to initiate the transplant process too soon. Flowering, leggy, or root-bound seedlings can experience stunting, and early production can be compromised. At five to six weeks before transplanting, sow at least 20 seeds in a row, ¼ inch deep in seal pack trays or flats of 20 rows. Alternatively, plant the tomatoes in 200-cell trays with one seed per cell, gently covered.

The seeding mix temperature should feature moderate moisture between 75–85°F. At the signs of the first true leaves, use four-inch pots or 50-cell trays and grow the tomatoes at a temperature between 60–70°F. After transplantation has occurred, grow the tomatoes at a constant temperature between 32–69°F with the addition of fertilizer treatments to harden them off.

Storage and harvesting

Tomatoes typically ripen from the blossom end to the shoulders and again from the base to the clusters and then the tips. Start to harvest the softer tomatoes into padded, shallow trays. Only the fruits that are fully ripe should be used at home or should be sold commercially to local grocery stores. The healthy but less ripe plants should be transported to locations further away. It's important to note that they will continue to ripen after being harvested.

Near-ripe and blemish-free tomatoes can be stored between four and seven days. Tomatoes mature once they are ready for transplantation.

Potential pests and diseases

The most annoying pests that tomatoes are exposed to are aphids, armyworms, bollworms, cutworms, leaf miners, red spider mites, root-knot nematodes, and thrips.

Cutworms, in particular, become a nuisance in seedbeds and pose the biggest threat to new transplants.

Containers

You need a container of at least one square foot (two squares is preferred) per plant. Five-gallon buckets are an ideal option for growing one tomato plant. Ensure the pot is filled with quality soil and the container has adequate drainage.

Fertilizer

Seedlings require a high-phosphate fertilizer during the planting phase to boost early production.

CHAPTER 17:
GROWING HERBS IN A GREENHOUSE

Greenhouse applications boast the ideal artificial growing environment to grow herbs. As a result, you can extend the growing season when the proper techniques are applied and significantly increase the varieties of herbs on your table.

Why Grow Herbs in a Greenhouse?

A greenhouse can control the shade, moisture, and heat, providing them with the perfect growing environment. In addition, cultivating herbs in greenhouses can protect annuals from the heat, permitting them to grow earlier and later than their natural seasons. The key lies in creating the perfect greenhouse environment before planting.

Which are the herbs to grow in a greenhouse?

Tender annuals are the best type of herbs to grow in a greenhouse. These include herb varieties that struggle to grow outside. Some of the most common herbs grown in a greenhouse include:

- basil
- chamomile
- chives
- cilantro
- dill
- mint
- parsley

Three Herbs to Grow in a Greenhouse

Below we will discuss the cultivation of three different herbs inside a greenhouse application.

Darki Parsley

Scientific Name: *Petroselinum crispum*

Description

There are many different types of parsley varieties. Some include Italian flat-leaf, curly-leaf, and root cultivars. Parsley has a sweet, clean aroma and flavor and is packed with essential minerals and vitamins such as potassium, calcium, and vitamin C. Parsley also has its uses for medicinal purposes, such as stimulating the body's digestive processes.

Plant uses

Parsley can be sprinkled on many dishes such as soups and picnic salads and is a much-loved staple in Italian homes, where *nonnas* use it for making a variety of pesto.

How to grow Darki parsley

For this specific purpose, we will use the Darki parsley variant. Darki parsley forms part of the curly-leaf varieties.

Germination time

Germination occurs between 14–30 days at a temperature ranging between 65–70°F.

Humidity

Parsley is a sturdy plant and can grow in various temperatures, although it prefers a humidity range between 50–70 degrees.

Temperature

Parsley requires the soil to be at least 70 degrees Fahrenheit to germinate.

Direct seeding requirements

It's best to sow parsley seeds after the frost season has passed. You can sow three seeds per row between ¼–½ inches deep. Alternatively, you can sow parsley in wide bands of two to three inches and between 12–18 inches apart. Thinner plants require to be sowed between eight and twelve inches apart.

Sowing

Plant the parsley seeds in one-inch cell containers.

Lighting

Parsley grows well in full lighting conditions and requires between six and eight hours of sunlight daily.

Water

Parsley plants prefer uniformly moist soil. Take care not to make the ground too soggy but to supply between one and two inches of water weekly. The soil should never dry out and quickly wither without sufficient water.

Soil pH

This crop prefers well-drained and loamy soil with a pH level between 6 and 7.

Transplanting

Parsley takes about three weeks to germinate. Once germination has occurred, they are ready for transplantation.

Storage and harvesting

Parsley is ready for harvesting once the crops are relatively bushy and six inches tall. Whole stems should be harvested from the plant base to promote further growth. Don't remove more than one-third of the leaves at any given time, and start harvesting parsley from the outer leaves until the inner leaves have reached maturity.

Fresh, harvested parsley stems should be kept in a container with water in the fridge and stay fresh for about seven days. One other method is to dry the leaves after cutting them. This can be done by hanging the leaves upside-down in a shady, warm spot that boasts good airflow. Once the leaves are dry, they should be placed in an airtight container.

Potential pests and diseases

The good news is that parsley crops are not predisposed to severe diseases. However, they are prone to fungal conditions such as damping off, leaf blights, leaf spot, powdery mildew, and septoria. This can be mitigated by sowing premium, disease-free seeds and planting them in an area with adequate air circulation.

The black swallowtail butterfly's caterpillar poses the most significant threat when it comes to pests. The parsley plant hosts these critters as the eggs hatch and the caterpillars munch on the leaves.

Containers

Growing parsley in containers is an excellent option if your garden has insufficient space. The ideal container is at least eight inches in width and depth, with enough drainage holes. When it comes to the material type of the container, an unglazed clay is a good option since this permits the surplus soil moisture to evaporate via the walls. Keep the water moisture constant and the plants exposed to the sun.

Fertilizer

Although it's not needed, parsley crops can benefit from fertilization once or twice during their growing season. Young seedlings can be treated once a month with a liquid fertilizer balanced at half-strength. Any fertilizer to be used needs to be targeted for use in edible plants. The other alternative to fertilizer would be to treat the soil with compost and organic matter.

Hera Dill

Scientific Name: *Anethum graveolens*

Description

Dill is also referred to as a dill weed plant, and the leaves are used for cooking purposes. The plant can be found in the spice aisle at commercial retailers and can be used fresh or dried.

Plant uses

Dill has a grassy licorice flavor used in *tzatziki* and ranch dressing dishes.

How to grow Hera Dill

For this specific purpose, we will use the Hera dill variant.

Temperature and humidity

Even though the optimal soil temperature for dill is 70 degrees Fahrenheit, it's a cold-hardy plant that can withstand temperatures as low as 25 degrees Fahrenheit.

Sowing

It's recommended to sow dill using the direct seeding method. The seeds should be sown in spring when the soil can be worked. Seeds should be planted between ⅛–¼ deep, approximately ¼–½ inches apart, in rows that are three inches apart. It's unnecessary to thin dill, and new seeds can be sown every third week to ensure continual fresh produce.

Germination

Germination of dill takes place between seven and 21 days after being sown.

Lighting

It's advisable to plant your dill in areas exposed to full sunlight daily, between six and eight hours per day. If you live where the climate is scorching in the summer months, the dill plants will enjoy some shade in the afternoon.

Water

Dill plants should be kept moist consistently, without becoming soaked or boggy, and should never dry out completely. The general rule of thumb is about one inch of water weekly.

Soil pH

Dill prefers a soil that is light but rich in nutrients with a pH level between 5.8–6.5. In addition, the ground should be well-draining. Dill is a self-sowing plant, so it needs to be planted where it can roam or where it will be harvested before reseeding.

Transplanting

Sow between three and five seeds in every cell using the cell tray method. Once the seedlings are ready for transplantation, you can plant them between two and four inches apart, in rows four inches apart.

Storage and harvesting

Dill is ready for harvesting once the plants start flowering. Take care to harvest the mature heads when they become golden brown.

Potential pests and diseases

Pests that threaten dill include root-nematodes, cutworms, armyworms, and aphids. Furthermore, dill is predisposed to diseases such as powdery mildew, downy mildew, and Cercospora leaf spot.

Containers

Dill can be grown indoors using cell trays or similar containers.

Fertilizer

If your soil is rich in organic matter, it's not needed to use additional fertilizer. Instead, the soil should be kept slightly on the lean side, yielding more aromatic plants.

Genovese Basil

Scientific Name: *Ocimum spp.*

Description

Genovese basil is a variety of basil that originates from Genoa, Italy. It is also known as sweet basil or Italian basil. This variety of basil is very popular in Italian cuisine and is often used to make pesto sauce. Genovese basil has large, dark green leaves and a strong, sweet flavor. It is one of the most commonly grown varieties of basil in North America.

Plant uses

Genovese basil is used in a variety of dishes, including pesto sauce, minestrone soup, and tomato-basil pasta. It can also be used to make homemade basil vinegar or oil. This type of basil has a strong flavor, so it is best used in cooked dishes rather than raw salads.

How to grow Genovese basil

For this specific purpose, we will use the Genovese basil variety.

Germination

Germination of basil transpires between five to ten days after being sown at temperatures ranging between 65-70°F.

Sowing

To grow basil, the direct seeding method is recommended. The seeds should be planted approximately ¼ inches deep, using two to three seeds per inch, in rows 18 inches apart. Once the seeds have been sown, gently firm the soil on top of the seeds. It's not necessary to thin basil but consider that a final spacing range between four and eight inches will yield full and healthy plants.

Humidity

The optimum humidity level for basil is between 40–60%.

Temperature

Basil prefers a temperature ranging between 50–80°F.

Lighting

To produce basil that matures well and yields healthy plants requires at least six to eight hours of full sunlight daily.

Water

Basil prefers to stay moist and requires the soil to be watered regularly and deeply, ensuring it drains well.

Soil pH

Basil thrives in moist, moderately-rich soil with a pH between 6.0–7.5.

Transplanting

Even though basil is a versatile plant, it's still as fragile as any young plant during transplantation. Before you even consider transplanting basil, ensure that the seedlings are strong enough to withstand the stresses of being transplanted. The general rule is to transplant basil five to six weeks after being sown. Some indicators that show your crops are ready to be transplanted include:

- with the appearance of the first true leaves
- when the seedlings are at least three inches in length
- when plant overcrowding can be observed

Furthermore, ensure that the seeds are sown indoors. During transplantation, replant the seeds with spacing between four and eight inches apart, with rows at least 18 inches in between.

Storage and harvesting

Your basil is ready to harvest once the seedlings have become established. It's recommended to facilitate this process in the early morning during cooler temperatures when leaves won't wilt.

Before the seedlings flower, the full harvesting process should be done by cutting the whole plant between four and six inches above the soil to establish the second growth phase.

Another important consideration is pinching the basil back frequently to produce bushes instead of growing lanky and tall. Basil is ready for pinching once the seedlings are about four inches tall. Always start with the top leaves while the bottom leaves are still maturing.

Be mindful that during the picking process, leaves are easily bruised, so they should be handled with care. Don't store the leaves in temperatures below 50°F. Basil can be used to make pesto and then frozen. A great use is to create a slurry by blending olive oil and basil and then freezing them into ice cubes.

Potential pests and diseases

Like any other houseplant, basil is predisposed to pests like aphids, mainly because they are grown indoors. Other potential problems include slugs and beetles when produced outdoors. To mitigate these critters, cover your plants with a soap solution. The quantities are two teaspoons of dishwashing liquid to one gallon of water.

Containers

The beauty of basil is that it can almost be cultivated in any container or pot. You can even go as far as using an old laundry basket or pre-used kiddies pool. Basil enjoys ample growth room, where air can circulate to the crops. A large pot is best to prevent the soil from completely drying out.

Fertilizer

When growing basil indoors, it doesn't really need additional fertilization. However, if you decide to boost your seedlings, adding a fertilizer every third or fourth week is advisable. Bear in mind that the solution should be very weak.

CHAPTER 18:
GROWING FRUITS IN A GREENHOUSE

When one thinks of growing produce in a greenhouse, the obvious choices like tomatoes and lettuce come to mind. But, certain fruits are just as beneficial to grow in greenhouses.

Why grow fruits in a greenhouse

Growing your own fruit and fruit trees in a greenhouse application is a healthy addition to any household. Nothing beats the feeling of going into your greenhouse and picking fresh, wholesome, and ripe fruit in the comfort of your own kitchen.

It's entirely possible to grow fruit in a greenhouse and allows you to cultivate species that might've not been possible to grow in your climate. So the only permutation to consider is setting up your greenhouse environment to this effect before sowing any seeds or planting any fruit trees.

Which are the best fruits to grow in a greenhouse?

Various fruit types thrive in a greenhouse application that is carefully monitored. The best piece of advice I can give here is to select fruit and fruit trees that love warm conditions, such as bananas, oranges, peaches, pears, and other tropical fruit. Conversely, fruit like apples won't work since they prefer a slight winter chill to grow.

Three Fruits to Grow in a Greenhouse

Below we will discuss the cultivation of three different fruit types in a greenhouse application.

Sparkle Strawberries

Scientific Name: _Fragaria spp._

Description

Interestingly, strawberries are considered accessory fruits and not part of the berry family. This is because the strawberry's delicious red flesh is laced with seeds (also called fruits or achenes).

Plant uses

Strawberries form part of the _Rosacea_ (rose) family, and with more than 20 different cultivars in existence, it's no wonder that it's the fruit of choice for dishes and beverages such as pasties, pies, malts, and smoothies.

How to grow Sparkle strawberries

For this specific purpose, we will use the Sparkle strawberry variant.

Sowing

Strawberry flower beds should be prepared in early spring on the previous fall to garner control over the occurrence of perennial weeds. The plants should be placed between 12 and 18 inches apart in rows three and four inches apart. The plants should be set down in the soil with the roots straight, ensuring the middle crown is level with the soil's top. Regular watering and weed maintenance are required. A mixture of mulch and straw is recommended during the late fall season to boost dormant plants. When the plants start growing, the same mulch must be pulled aside in spring. The mulch can then be left on the footpaths to help suppress weeds and keep the fruit clean.

Germination time

The germination of strawberries can take between seven days and six weeks. Patience is key here. As soon as germination has transpired, the air ventilation around the crops needs to be increased to prevent damping off.

Humidity

The plants require a daytime humidity level between 65–75% to provide a good strawberry yield.

Temperature

Strawberries require clean, unobstructed windows to allow maximum light to seep through. In addition, the crops require an optimal temperature no lower than 60°F until flowering has occurred.

Lighting

Strawberry crops need full sun, warmth, and light to grow for at least six hours daily.

Water

These plants feature shallow root systems. To obtain the maximum yield and growth, ensure the plants are never stressed by water absence. Newly set strawberries should be well-irrigated and require rain and supplemental irrigation between 0.98–1.37 inches weekly.

Soil pH

Strawberry crops thrive in a partially shaded to a sunny site in well-draining and moist soil. Furthermore, they prefer an ideal soil pH range between 6.5–6.8.

Transplanting

Young strawberry seedlings are ready for transplantation once they develop their third true leaf. Gently transplant each seedling into its own pot. It's advisable to harden off all seedlings before they are transplanted outside. Do this daily at a gradual pace a few weeks before transplantation transpires.

Storage and harvesting

Strawberries are generally ready between four and six weeks after they blossom. Therefore, it's vital only to pick the fully red (ripe) berries and to pick them in cycles every third day. Harvest the plants by cutting them from the stem. Don't pull on the actual berry, as this may damage the whole plant.

Strawberries can be kept for up to seven days after being harvested. Cool the berries between 32–34°F to prevent them from decaying or overripening.

Potential pests and diseases

Some diseases relating to strawberry plants include angular leaf spot, mucor fruit rot, leaf blotch, and verticillium wilt. Unfortunately, some pesky critters love to munch on these yummy plants. Some creatures include strawberry leafrollers, sap beetles, chili thrips, and tarnished plant bugs.

Containers

Some containers that are ideal for the cultivation of strawberries include:

- Bespoke strawberry planters
- hanging baskets
- growing bags
- pop-up trugs on legs
- terracotta pots, and
- window boxes

Fertilizer

Strawberries should receive at least one treatment every season with a naturally acid mixture of 4–3–6. Fertilization should only be done just before harvest time to avoid too soft strawberries that will easily rot.

Blueberries

Scientific Name: *Vaccinium corymbosum*

Description

These tiny blue-black berries are edible and grow in clusters in the North-American regions. It's related to the bilberry.

Plant uses

These berries have a sweet taste with an acid undertone. They are commonly used in baking and staple food items such as muffins, pancakes, and smoothies.

How to grow blueberries

Germination time

Blueberry seeds will germinate approximately one month after being sown. The seedlings that will emerge are tiny in stature.

Humidity

Blueberries prefer a relative humidity level ranging between 85–90%.

Temperature

Blueberries are resilient crops and can tolerate temperatures ranging from -20°C to -5°F without damage. However, should the plants become snow-covered, ensure that the roots are well-protected with a winter cover such as mulch. This way, they can withstand even lower temperatures.

Planting

Plants should be spaced between four and five inches apart. The plants should be set in holes one by one inch in diameter, covering the roots up to the natural soil line. During the first year, all the flowers should be removed during the first year before berries manifest. Removing the flowers will ensure the plant's energy is sent to the shoots and roots. In the first several growth years, pruning won't be needed.

Lighting

Blueberries require between six and eight hours of daily sunlight (directly).

Water

During the growth and summer seasons, these crops need plenty of moisture. Blueberries feature a shallow root system that is susceptible to drought. In the absence of adequate water supply, blueberries can be sensitive to lower yields and dwarf growth or death. While blueberries don't like dry soil, they also don't prefer soil that is too soggy either.

Soil pH

These crops thrive in a location boasting full sun and moist, acidic soil. The optimal pH soil level is 4.8.

Transplanting

Blueberry transplantation should occur when the plant has become dormant, which is usually once the majority of the frost season has occurred.

Storage and harvesting

Once the berries have turned blue, they are ready for harvest. The typical harvest season lasts between six and eight weeks. However, it's important to note that blueberries mature at different times and in various stages. Therefore, it's crucial not to rush or damage the plant when picking ripe berries.

After harvesting has transpired, the berries can be kept in plastic containers and held in the fridge for three to four weeks at an ideal temperature of 33°F.

Blueberries for at-home consumption should be eaten immediately to avoid the loss of aroma and fragrance.

Potential pests and diseases

Fungal diseases that blueberries are prone to include gray mold, mummy berry, powdery mildew, shoestring, and stem canker. Blueberries are also predisposed to contract oomycete diseases such as phytophthora root rot.

Potential blueberry pests to look out for include the blueberry bud mite, flea beetle, Japanese beetle, sharp-nosed leafhopper, and thrips.

Containers

It's best to grow blueberries in large weather-resistant, well-draining pots, such as wooden barrel planters. Fully-grown blueberries need a pot at least between 24–30 inches in width and 24 inches in depth. Smaller bushes should first be planted in smaller pots and then transplanted as they grow into larger pots or flower beds.

Fertilizer

It's recommended to fertilize blueberries before their leaves start to grow. This provides the fertilizer solution with sufficient time to absorb the nutrients. Blueberry fertilizer works best when applied before the active growth stage in the summer months. Therefore, new blueberry seedlings should be fed once in early and once in late spring.

Sorbet Watermelon

Scientific Name: *Citrullus lanatus var. lanatus*

Description

Botanically watermelon is known as a *pepo* and falls under the berry family. Its juicy and sweet flesh can be red, yellow, or white. The shape, size, and rind thickness depend on the watermelon type being grown.

Plant uses

Watermelon is a versatile summer dish used in fruit salads, ice lollies, or enjoyed ice-cold on its own.

How to grow Sorbet watermelon

For this specific purpose, we will use the Sorbet watermelon variety.

Germination time

Watermelon seeds take between four to 12 days to germinate.

Humidity

Watermelon plants prefer a humidity level ranging between 80–95%.

Temperature

The best temperature to grow watermelon ranges between 35–50 degrees Fahrenheit.

Sowing (direct seeding)

Watermelon seeds should be sown between one and two weeks after the last frost has occurred when the soil temperature is higher than 70°F. Ideally, seeds must be implanted in groups of three every 18–36 inches and between ½ to one inch deep in the soil. Thinning should transpire by planting one plant per spot.

Lighting

Watermelons require ample sunshine. They have a daily direct sunlight requirement of six to eight hours. When aluminum foil is placed underneath the watermelon plants, they will ripen quicker. When watermelon crops are in good health, they can yield two to four melons per plant.

Water

From sowing until fruit-formation for watermelon plants, adequate watering measures are required. While in the growing phase, watermelons require between one and two inches of water weekly. The soil should be moist but shouldn't become soggy or waterlogged.

Soil pH

Watermelons require an optimal soil pH between 6.5–7.5 in the form of well-drained, light soil in the southern part of the greenhouse. Proper soil moisture is essential during the early growth and pollination stages as the fruit sets. Water feeding should be ceased approximately one week before ripening since overwatering can produce bland fruits.

Transplanting

Watermelon should be sown indoors in 50-cell plug trays or peat pots ranging between two to three inches. Sowing should take place at least four weeks before transplantation occurs. Ideally, two seeds per cell should be sown approximately ½–1 inch in depth. The optimum temperature range to grow watermelon should be between 80–90°F until they germinate. It's also important to never allow the soil to dry out.

Seedlings should be grown at 75°F. Before transplantation, the temperature should be reduced, together with the water content, to harden–off the seedlings in preparation for the transplantation phase. Once the weather is warm enough, the young seedlings should be transplanted two to three inches apart in rows separated by six to eight inches. Alternatively, thin one plant per cell with scissors and transplant about 18 inches apart. It's important to note that even the most healthy watermelon seedlings are tender. Therefore it's important not to disturb their roots during transplantation and to ensure that they are appropriately watered after transplantation.

Storage and harvesting

When harvest time comes, watermelon must be cut at the stems with a gardening tool. Never pull the plant from the actual vine, as this can cause damage. Signs of watermelon maturity will differ according to the cultivar. However, the general rule of thumb is that watermelons are generally ripe when they sound hollow when being "knocked on." After sowing, watermelons are ready about ten days after the direct seeding method has been used.

After harvesting watermelons, they can be kept at 45°F at a relative humidity level of 85% for up to three weeks. It's important to note that whole watermelons will stay fresher when stored at room temperature in a dark, cool place to prevent further ripening. The shelf life of picked watermelons can be extended by three weeks when held at a temperature range between 50 to 60 degrees Fahrenheit. Once a watermelon is fully ripe, it will only last up to seven days before it becomes overripe.

Potential pests and diseases

The disease that watermelons are most prone to is called "sudden wilt." This is a tricky disease brought on by the sudden onset of cold weather, and this can cause premature ripeness, meaning plants can wilt overnight.

Critters that love to munch on watermelon include cucumber beetles. These insects can be kept at bay by investing in floating row covers during the transplantation or by controlling them using insecticide application.

Containers

Picking the right pot for your watermelon is vital for their growth. An optimal container will have a depth of two feet and a width of at least one foot. Due to the long taproot system of watermelon crops, they require a deep container featuring adequate drainage.

Fertilizer

Watermelon requires phosphorus-rich fertilizer with a range of 10–10–10. Fertilizer can be fed at four pounds to every 1,000 square feet. Dig a trench on the plant bed between four and six inches in depth and about two inches from each row's side. The plant and the fertilizer should be covered so that the fertilizer doesn't come into contact with the watermelon seeds.

Chapter 19:
Growing Flowering Plants in a Greenhouse

Did you know that certain flower types also thrive in a greenhouse application? With today's advanced technology in the arena, you can now grow beautiful blooms all-year-round ranging from tropical flowers to everyday blooms such as sunflowers.

Why Grow Flowers in a Greenhouse

There are many benefits attached to growing flowers in a greenhouse environment. Some advantages include:

- All-weather gardening.
- Adequate protection against diseases and pests.
- Going green to benefit the environment.

Which are the Best Flowers to Grow in a Greenhouse?

A list of typical greenhouse-grown flowers include species such as:

- Caladiums
- Chrysanthemums
- Coleus
- Ferns
- Gazanias
- Geraniums
- Impatiens
- Pansies
- Petunias
- Poinsettias
- Salvia

Three Flowers to Grow in a Greenhouse

Below we will discuss in detail the cultivation of three common greenhouse plants.

Frizzle-Sizzle Yellow-Blue Swirl Viola (Pansy)

Scientific Name: *Viola spp*

Description

Other names that violas are known by include European field pansy, Johnny-jump-up, heart's ease, and hybrid violet. Pansies are cool-seasoned flowers. There are over 600 different species of violas in existence.

Plant uses

Violas are edible flowers and form part of the cut variety. They are excellent plants to grow in garden beds or pots. The pansy type planted will depend on factors such as temperature and the raised area.

How to grow Frizzle-Sizzle Yellow-Blue Swirl violas

We will use the Frizzle-Sizzle Yellow-Blue Swirl pansy example for this specific purpose.

Germination time

Violas germinate between four and seven days at a temperature between 62–68°F.

Humidity

Pansies thrive in an environment with a relative humidity of 62%.

Temperature

These plants enjoy the cooler temperatures in early spring and will grow in temperatures between 40–70 degrees Fahrenheit.

Sowing

Violas should be sown between eight and nine weeks ahead of blooming if they will be grown in cell packs. Seeds are to be covered lightly once planted.

Lighting

Pansies prefer a balance of sun and partial shade. However, they thrive in indirect sunlight for between six and eight hours daily.

Water

During the watering process, take care to water pansies either from the bottom or only mist them gently on top to avoid overwatering the seeds and possibly displacing them. Violas require approximately one inch of moisture weekly. Take care not to leave the soil soggy.

Soil pH

Violas need moist, well-draining, and rich soil with an acidic pH level between 5.4–6.2.

Transplanting

Pansies are ready for transplanting between seven and nine weeks after being sown. Violas should be transplanted into large pots or cell packs as soon as the true leaves manifest. The plants should be hardened off before transplantation occurs.

Storage and harvesting

Edible pansies are ready for harvest as soon as the plants are in full bloom and before they start to wilt. Cut the stems during the cooler parts of the day. This way, you will ensure they retain the highest moisture level, which will keep them looking perky and fresh. Ideally, if possible, the flowers should be harvested just before use.

Violas can be stored in an airtight container in the fridge between four and six days.

Potential pests and diseases

Another great thing about pansies is that they are pretty hardy regarding potential threats from pests and diseases. In the occurrence of pests or diseases, these issues can be mitigated using chemical or organic fungicides and repellents. Some critters and diseases that tend to manifest include crown and root rot and insects such as aphids, spider mites, and slugs.

Containers

Pansies are versatile enough to be grown in almost any container or pot, permitting a depth of at least four inches. However, the flowering violas prefer to have some growth room, so planting one young sprout for each six to eight inches of pot space is advisable. The other planting option is to grow each pansy into its own four-inch container with well-draining capabilities.

Fertilizer

Pansies can benefit from a small dose of fertilizer (organic) once monthly during the growing season.

Giant Yellow Marigold

Scientific Name: *Tagetes spp.*

Description

Marigolds originally come from Mexico and form part of the sunflower family. There are approximately 50 different types of marigolds in existence.

Plant uses

With the bright and cheerful hues that marigold flowers come in, it's no wonder that no garden is complete without adding these blooming beauties.

How to grow Giant Yellow marigold

For this specific purpose, we will use the Giant Yellow variant. Marigolds are also edible plants with various uses in sweet and savory dishes.

Germination time

The plant germinates between four to seven days after being sown.

Humidity

This marigold variety requires about 90% relative humidity until the seedlings emerge.

Temperature

The ideal temperature to grow this marigold variety ranges between 75–80°F (24-27°C).

Sowing

It's recommended that after sowing, these plants need to be transplanted. Start by sowing seeds into 72-cell (flat) seedling containers. The ideal time to sow is four to six weeks after the last frost has fallen. Cover the seeds gently with soil.

Direct seeding method

The best time to use the direct seeding method is after the last frost has transpired. Sow each seed approximately ¼ in deep, and remember that pinching promotes branching.

Lighting

Marigolds thrive when they obtain a full day's sun. This means that six hours daily is sufficient, but eight hours are preferred.

Water

Once the marigold seedlings are established, they will require a proper soak weekly. The key is to supply sufficient moisture for the soil to be moist at a depth between six and eight inches. However, if the climate is very hot or windy. When to water is judged by when the top one to two inches of soil is no longer moist.

Soil pH

Marigolds prefer an average soil type with a pH between 6.0–7.5.

Transplanting

Young marigold seedlings should be hardened off and transplanted after the last frost. When using flowering in a pack, sow the seeds about eight weeks before the preferred bloom time.

Storage and harvesting

The ideal time to harvest marigolds is when the blooms are open at capacity, and the centers are still tight.

Potential pests and diseases

Some of the most prevalent diseases that marigolds are prone to include blight, mildew, and rot. These plant illnesses manifest during warm and wet conditions when fungal spores are at their most widespread. This can be mitigated by avoiding overhead watering, which halts the spread and formation of spores.

Potential marigold pests to look out for include Aphids, caterpillars, Earwigs, Leafminers, slugs, snails, Spider Mites, Thrips, and Whiteflies.

Containers

Some containers that work well with marigolds include beds, borders, containers, mass plantings, and window boxes.

Fertilizer

Marigolds should be fed fertilizer employing a slow-release product with an NPK of 11–40–6. Fertilizers should be provided between seven and ten days after being set out at the start of spring. Use approximately one teaspoon of fertilizer per plant for returning perennial marigold varieties.

California Poppy

Scientific Name: *Eschscholzia californica*

Description

This brightly-colored bloom became the state of California's official flower on March 2, 1903. The diamond-petaled variant is one of California's rarest plants. There are over 120 known species of poppy worldwide today.

Plant uses

Poppies are a flower used in the production of drugs (codeine and morphine) due to their opium content. Furthermore, poppy oil is manufactured for use on human skin, and the seeds are commonly used in cooking.

How to grow California Poppies

For this specific purpose, we will use the California Poppy variant.

Germination time

This poppy variant takes between 14 and 21 days to germinate.

Humidity

California poppies prefer a humidity level that ranges between 50–75 °F. As long as the humidity level is mid-range, this flower will continue to grow. When it becomes too hot, the plant may become dormant or stagnant, but as soon as the temperature returns to normal, it's been found that poppies will regrow and even rebloom.

Temperature

Poppies tend to grow and bloom during the daytime temperature when the climate is between 50–80°F.

Sowing

It's best to sow California poppies by deploying the direct seeding method. Once the last frost has dissipated, sow the poppy seeds and cover them with about ¼ in of soil. Thin the seedlings 6 inches apart to stand when the first true leaves have appeared. The flowers will thrive in the cooler nights and will bloom freely.

Lighting

Poppies require full sun (between six and eight hours daily).

Water

California poppies are relatively low–maintenance when it comes to watering. In fact, poppies prefer supplemental moisture every four to eight weeks in clay soil during cooler months and bi-weekly in warmer weather.

Soil pH

These flowers prefer a neutral to acidic soil type with an ideal pH range of 6.5–7.5.

Transplanting

When transplanting California poppies, sow them two to three weeks after the last frost into the desired containers or cell packs. Gently cover the seeds with the growing medium. Mist or provide moisture from the bottom. Gradually harden the seedlings off a few weeks before transplantation is due, and once the frost dangers have subsided.

Harvesting

California poppies are best harvested when the flowers are in full bloom.

Potential pests and diseases

Poppies are prone to plant diseases such as Tomato spotted wilt virus, powdery mildew, downy mildew, and gray mold.

Common poppy pests include Black Bean aphids, Melon aphids, True bugs, and Hoplia beetles.

Containers

Any container in a medium size will be suitable for growing California poppies, providing that the container has never been exposed to any chemicals. The pot needs adequate drainage to avoid the seedlings standing in soggy soil.

Fertilizer

California poppies are one of the few flower varieties that don't need any fertilizer. The same rule even applies to areas where the soil quality is inferior. Feeding the poppies additional chemicals will result in overgrown foliage with no blooms.

Next up: A yearly planting calendar.

CHAPTER 20:
YEAR-ROUND GREENHOUSE PLANTING CALENDAR

There's much garden maintenance and deadlines to ensure you harvest the right plants at the desired times. To make life easier, I'd recommend using a planting calendar. Let's take a look at this in more detail.

Planting Calendar Definition and Uses

In simple terms, a planting calendar is a schedule; a growing guide of sorts to when what needs to happen in each phase of your individual plant's growth cycle. These systems are designed to provide information at your fingertips, such as when to sow seeds, water requirements, and harvesting information based on each month.

Disclaimer: The information set out below is based on the plant growing requirements of the United States Northern Hemisphere territories

A Typical Year-Round Planting Calendar

February

During the second month of the year, the days are getting longer as the Earth moves closer to the celestial equator. It's also when we receive up to 10 hours of daily sunlight and marks the start of the new seed sowing process, sans supplemental lighting systems.

In February, the first round of cold-tolerant and spring crops can be seeded. Examples include beets, carrots, kale, lettuce, peas, and radishes.

You can also start to seed long-season, warm-loving veggies in your greenhouse, such as eggplant, peppers, and tomatoes. These heatseekers usually take between 100 and 150 days to reach maturity and don't like the colder temperatures. So, the idea is to give them the most time in a heat–controlled environment until their fruit ripens.

Start by planting the seeds in your structure and prepare them for transplantation-when the temperature at night is 55 degrees fahrenheit and above consistently. Alternatively, you can opt to keep them in the greenhouse the whole summer to mid-fall.

You'll also use this time to prepare for the upcoming spring season by seeding carrots, salad leaves, and spinach. These plants will be ready for harvest at the start of the new season.

If you are a potato grower, you will now be chitting your potatoes (helping them sprout before planting them).

March to April

As we approach spring equinox time, the days will be longer, and the plants will start developing quicker in your greenhouse. Now is the time to sow all your warm-season plants that take a shorter time to mature. Examples of such crops include squash, cucumbers, basil, and beans).

During these two months, you will also start to harvest the first available yields from your cold-tolerant plants. As you harvest, you will immediately plant again to replace the ones that have been picked.

March

Most of March will be spent planting veg with large leaves and seeds. They will be grown in individual containers before being placed into a propagator. The crops will be ready to move approximately 30 days after being sown in their pots.

For a quick turnaround this month, sow a tray heavily with peas and ensure they receive water daily.

It's also time to plant the broad bean variety (if that tickles your fancy). Plant them in cardboard tubes to enable easier transplantation. Check the moisture levels frequently and turn the containers to ensure the beans don't bend or turn while growing.

Author's Top Tips

A. Remember that with spring, you can expect vast climate fluctuations relevant to your greenhouse. I suggest keeping your greenhouse air temperature at a range of 45–64°F during nighttime. On the sunnier days ensure that damping down and ventilation is applied.

B. As March progresses, open the vents and doors more regularly to prevent plant diseases and to keep humidity levels in check.

April

April earmarks the time to sow plants like carrots and peas outside, but still, use your greenhouse to grow the more tender plants such as courgettes and aubergines.

May

May is a magical time as you will enjoy a growth spurt amongst your plants with the longer days and warmer evenings.

You can typically expect to start harvesting yields from plants like peas, spinach, kale, and lettuce.

You might also have transplanted some crops in your greenhouse. This means that your cold-tolerant plants can be transplanted outdoors. Some examples include cabbage, cauliflower, and broccoli. You'll know the time is right when the evening temperatures are above 45 degrees at a constant pace.

It's also time to take your warm-season crops outside and initiate the transplantation process (eggplant, peppers, and tomatoes). Ensure that the evening temperatures are above 55 degrees first, though.

If you are a lover of French beans, then they can now be sown inside the greenhouse. These crops need warmth to facilitate germination and don't like frost. After four to six weeks have lapsed, they can be moved to raised garden beds.

Sweetcorn lovers will delight that they can now sow these plants in preparation for buttery corn on the cob for those long, lazy summer BBQs.

You can also use this time to plan for a yield of kale by starting the seeds in the greenhouse during this month.

June to July

During June and July, the temperatures outside will soar, and your all-important cooling systems will come into play. All the while checking for overheating, you will enjoy yields from plants such as tomatoes, peppers, eggplant, and beans.

Double-check your greenhouse ventilation and ensure the relevant humidity levels are achieved to keep your plants happy and healthy.

June

June is the midway mark for our annual greenhouse planting calendar and the time to plant peas. Pea plants should be kept in the greenhouse until they shoot to avoid luring mice. I suggest making drainage holes before planting them in yogurt containers or newspaper pots.

July

July is for planting winter lettuce varieties such as Veneziana and Winter Density inside the greenhouse. A recycled ice cream tub is perfect as a starter pot. However, they would need to be separated later in the same month to give them sufficient growth space.

August to September

The time has come to focus on preparing your winter greenhouse crops. It's imperative to remember that between November and January, the days become shorter, and your plants will require supplemental lighting systems to grow at their optimum.

The idea of winter greenhouse yields is to sow and seed crops early enough so that most of them mature by November/December. Plants will experience a phase of semi-hibernation. This means you must start picking your ripe produce during winter, even though the new growth cycle might appear slow initially.

It's crucial to move your plants in containers inside the greenhouse before the first frost falls. Potted plants like tomatoes, peppers, figs, and citrus fruit can't withstand the cold winter temperatures outside. When moved inside, the same crops in containers can survive and produce fruits for three consecutive seasons when cared for.

August

If you are looking for a colorful crop to brighten the autumn blues, then swiss chard is the answer. Sow varieties such as Magenta Sunset and Bright Lights for the best results.

September

For the greenies that like the weird and wonderful, try your hand at growing tatsoi– similar to cabbages with a more delicate flower and easier to cultivate. Some caution is advised since tatsoi must be sown when the days are cooler and shorter to avoid bolting. Bolting will make the leaves taste bitter.

October

By October, the days are getting shorter; your winter crops should be seeded/sowed by now. If you haven't done so already, don't fret! October still provides sufficient daylight to start plants that mature quickly (such as radishes that take a mere 20–30 days until ready for harvest).

You can also use this time to harvest early spring/late winter crops to allow them to grow slowly during the winter.

October is also when your hardy veggies such as kale, lettuce, and spinach germinate and transform into seedlings. They typically experience a growth spurt when the days become longer around February.

During this period, early spring and winter veggies have a sweeter palate than other times of the year as they harbor sugars in the cell walls to shield them from the possible onslaught of frost.

Herb gardeners unite! October is the perfect time to start your herb garden endeavors. Plant crops such as basil, chives, and dill ready to use in your kitchen come winter.

Two other spring crops to consider planting at this time are cauliflower and spring onion. Both can be grown inside the greenhouses under cloches and will be ready for picking in the spring.

November to January

Use these last three months to decide if you want to replant the same crops or introduce different varieties into your greenhouse. By now, your greenhouse should look pretty empty, and you can also catch a much-needed break from intensive gardening.

From November to January, you can slowly but surely harvest from the matured crops and invest your time doing gardening chores such as cutting spinach, digging beets and carrots, and even pulling off kale leaves. Remember also to take some time to prune your fruit-bearing trees and finalize what to plant for the next growing season. Reflect, and plan for the year ahead.

If you use supplemental lighting, you will have a very different picture in your greenhouse during this time. You'll find the inside of your structure awash with root veggies and leafy greens that love a winter environment with the added benefit of additional light.

November

The time has come to harvest and plant microgreens. In short, microgreens are mini versions of the parent plant. They are cut when each plant starts producing its first leaves that resemble a parent plant. Some examples that can be planted and harvested include beetroot, coriander, rocket, and spinach.

Author's Top Tip

It's best to harvest microgreens with a pair of scissors over a period of one week. These microgreens must be resown frequently to keep stock levels throughout the winter.

December

By now, you are probably using heating systems inside your greenhouse. It's also time for crops like chilies, peppers, and tomatoes.

If you don't use heating systems, you can use the time to prepare your greenhouse to plant veggies, herbs, and salads for next year and look at some possible shelving options.

January

You will use most of January to sow oriental greens and hardy salad crops such as pak choi and mustard greens.

Remember to pinch and transplant crops like onions and sweet peas into larger containers.

Author's Top Tip

You can add compost for potting and sowing into the greenhouse a few days before using it. This will heat the compost and ensure it doesn't chill seedlings and young crops.

Supplemental Information

I have also used my winter greenhouse to grow crops that like warm weather, such as peppers and tomatoes. I used supplemental lighting during the winter when my greenhouse temperature dropped to less than 62 degrees. This was made possible by erecting a structure that harvests daylight from the reflecting north, east and west walls. This means my crops needed fewer supplemental lighting aid in the winter and still grew strong.

You might be wondering what *your* specific planting calendar or schedule will look like. The good news is that any growth consultants employed by a reputable company will support and guide you through a customizable planting schedule, including the factors you need to consider.

Fundamental Factors to Consider

Of course, there are various factors to consider when planning your planting calendar or schedule. Notably, two elements, in particular, are of utmost importance, namely:

- day length
- temperature

Day length

Day length, in particular, is probably the singular most important aspect when it comes to drafting your greenhouse planting schedule. Should you decide not to go with supplemental lighting, it's imperative that you plant around the various day lengths for your region.

For instance, in the Northern US territories where I live, February is when we experience about 10 hours of light a day, which is ideal for seedling growth. Conversely, around the middle of November, crop growth slows, and we have less than 10 hours of daily sunlight.

Temperature

The second factor to plan around is maintaining the ideal growing temperature in your greenhouse application (bear in mind the microclimates also play a role).

The plants planted near the glazing and the vents will experience cooler temperatures than the rest of the structure. I'd recommend planting your cold-tolerant veggies like kale and spinach here. On the other hand, the north-facing wall will be the warmest part of your structure.

Deploying these two factors into your planning will allow you to pick the right crop varieties to ensure farm-to-table goodness throughout the year. The temperature inside the greenhouse can be regulated by alternating heating and cooling systems.

With that being said, let's move onto greenhouse maintenance information.

CHAPTER 21:
GREENHOUSE MAINTENANCE, UPKEEP, AND PEST CONTROL

Now that we've covered the best part, we have to move onto how to maintain your greenhouse to get the most out of your crops and harvests.

<u>**Some factors we will discuss in this chapter include:**</u>

- maintenance issues
- pests
- plant diseases
- cleaning

Pests

Why do bugs manifest in a greenhouse? The humid and warm climate and abundant food sources create the perfect environment for pests to develop and thrive. This is in addition to the threat of outside enemies being neutralized when they live inside the structure. For precisely these reasons, pest conditions often proliferate in a greenhouse much faster than outdoors. Bug issues can become chronic unless identified and correctly mitigated.

If a workable pest management system is not implemented, you and your greenhouse can suffer significant losses. Successful control over plant pests will involve steps such as:

- Deploying the appropriate cultural practices will decrease the chances of bugs appearing and causing possible infestations.
- Early identification and diagnosis.
- The right choice of pesticides and alternative de-infestation measures.

These bugs don't only attack your crops but also float systems. Float systems are predisposed and sensitive to pests such as bloodworms, fungus gnats, and shore flies.

Moreover, some greenhouse bugs carry diseases to the crops that can cause more harm than just feeding holes in the plants. Some disease-carrying pests include whiteflies, thrips, leafhoppers, and aphids.

Because some pests are much harder to keep in tow than others, it's of vital importance that regular pest maintenance and overall greenhouse monitoring are often performed.

Common Greenhouse Pests and Controlling Them

There are many different types of greenhouse pests. They can be divided into three categories, namely:

- Caterpillars and slugs
- Pollen feeders
- Sap-feeders

Let's look at them in closer detail.

Caterpillars and Slugs

Even though their appearance is occasional, their onslaught is still severe in a greenhouse.

Plant Damages Caused

They are commonly classified as defoliators, and they are drawn to the succulent and tender growing crops and will chew on your young plants until there's nothing left.

The only real sign of these critters is the crop leaves resembling skeletons and appearing to be chewed from the outside.

Pest Control Actions

These bugs can be hand-picked from your plants and thrown in a bucket containing a water and soap solution. When looking for the pests, be sure to check underneath benches and shelves and also to remove any debris they leave behind. It's crucial to get this type of infestation as soon as possible, as the damage can quickly spin out of control.

Pollen Feeders

A pollen-feeding insect is a bug that forages on the pollen that contains vital nutrients produced by the plant's gymnosperms and angiosperms. They also go by the zoology name of *Palynivores*. For this book, we will delve into detail on fungus gnats, shore flies, and thrips.

Fungus Gnats

This is a tiny fly that frequents greenhouses. They infest mediums such as organic compost, potting mix, and soil.

Plant damages caused

Some good news is that only the larvae threaten plants, while the adults are just a nuisance. The larvae chomp on overwatered plant roots.

Signs of infestation

The first indication of a fungus gnat infestation will often include a bunch of adults swarming around freshly or over watered crop containers and decaying organic material (compost). The larvae are especially cunning in that they hide away as deep as two to three inches in the soil. Even though they aren't immediately visible, you can recognize a plant problem by means of wilted plants or those suffering from stunted growth. As the larvae chomp on the plant roots, this promotes rot, making even more food for the larvae at the expense of your crops.

Pest control actions

Effective management of this pest includes taking action at soil surface level to dispel existing larvae and before new adults have a chance to manifest and mature. Place the affected containers outside. Apply a generous amount of insecticide spray over all container surfaces, and allow it to dry completely before bringing the container back inside. Invest in a reputable pest-killing brand such as *GardenTech®* , whose products are known to provide effective control for up to three months.

Shore flies

Shore flies and fungus gnats are both small flies, but shore flies are sturdier in appearance. Shore flies also love moist greenhouse conditions. These pests manifest during the plug production, plant propagation phases, and just before roots establish.

Plant damages caused

To reiterate, this pest doesn't actually consume greenhouse crops. So other than visible damage, they are more an eyesore than anything else as they destroy the aesthetic value of your plants.

Signs of infestation

In the instance of a heavy shore fly infestation, you'll notice black specks on crop leaves. Even though they are unsightly, there is no further cause for concern. Interestingly enough, shore fly larvae feed on algae and not on plants. However, adult shore flies are known to transmit diseases to crop roots.

Pest control actions

By limiting algae growth, adequate shore fly control can be achieved. There are many ways to control this pest infestation. Two methods include using less fertilizer and not overwatering crops. Furthermore, repairing leaks in irrigation systems and hoses and removing standing water as much as possible.

You can also perform shore fly control by scrubbing algae from surfaces such as benches, floors, gutters, and walls. I personally use a steam cleaner for the best results. If you are set on getting rid of shore flies for good, you may want to use an insecticide. The challenging part is that you'd have to use two different types. You need an insecticide for the larvae and an insecticide for the adults since the adulticide won't work on the larvae.

Thrips

Thrips are also referred to as thunder flies and resemble a fat needle–like structure with wings that suck on crops.

Plant damages caused

The real damage is caused by transmitting viruses to the plants. You might also notice stunted flower and fruit growth.

Signs of infestation

Unfortunately, they are pretty tricky to spot. A thunder fly infestation can be identified by means of minute dark slivers on crops. Their bodies are hard to see without using a magnifying glass. Up close, they resemble lobsters. Take a sheet of printing paper and shake the bugs off to see them properly.

Pest control actions

Here, you can use blue or yellow sticky tape. Furthermore, you could shake the pests from the plant leaves on a cloth for quick removal. Infestation on fruit trees can be controlled by spraying dormant oil on the leaves. In addition (but only as a last resort), you could apply a dusting of diatomaceous earth.

Sap-Feeders

These critters are found on the leaves, roots, and stems-aphids munch on plants' sap (phloem). As a result, they leave weak plants and sticky honeydew in their wake. The difference between sap-feeders and ants and beetles is that these pests have a mouth comprising piercing and sucking parts. At first, it can be challenging to spot sap feeder damage. The first sign of infestation includes a sheen and a sticky feel to the leaves. Over time, the sticky plants could turn dark and will feature a mold that is sooty in color. This mold is a fungus that develops on the sugar of drippy droppings of the sap feeder.

For this book, we will unpack sap feeders such as aphids, mites, and whiteflies.

Aphids

Aphids are tiny green insects with soft bodies. They suck all of the nutrients from the crop's liquids, and in swarms they can harm fruits and flowers and weaken plants in the process. What makes aphids so dangerous is their ability to proliferate in a short amount of time. Therefore it's vital to control an infestation before their reproduction phase, as many aphid generations can transpire in only one season.

Plant damages caused

Signs of damage include curled, deformed, stunted or yellow leaves. You could also expect to see deformed or distorted fruits and flowers in addition to galls on leaves and roots.

Signs of infestation

Apart from the symptoms mentioned above, you could also expect a sugary, sticky honeydew to manifest on crop leaves. This means that the aphids have been sipping on the sap of your plants.

Pest control actions

There are various minimally invasive and eco-friendly aphid pest control options. Methods include:

- **Spraying infested crops with a strong water stream** to dislodge the bugs. The chances are they will return. This can be mitigated by utilizing insecticidal soaps and neem oil.
- **Dehydrating the aphids** by dusting crop leaves with diatomaceous earth.
- **Attracting beneficial insects to your garden**, such as ladybugs that feed on aphids.
- **Planting companion plants** that will keep aphids at bay, such as catnip.
- **Creating a solution of rubbing alcohol and water.** Use a 95 percent alcohol mix with an equal part of water.

Author's Top Tip

Don't spray the solution over the entire plant in one sitting when using any spraying medium mentioned above. Instead, gently wipe or spray only on the affected areas. Lastly, bear in mind that repeat applications might be needed.

Mites

Did you know that mites are part of the arachnid family? In fact, they are a relative of spiders. They also have eight legs, with a body segmented into two parts. It's tough to diagnose mites on crops due to their diminutive stature.

Plant damages caused

These bugs and their destruction are versatile. They transmit some notable diseases and viruses and also decrease crop vigor.

Signs of infestation

They feed on the crop cells by piercing them and then sucking on the inside liquids. This action will leave plant leaves with yellow spots or necrosis. One classic sign of mite infestation is speckled foliage. Furthermore, you might also notice cobwebs on your plants. Now, if you've been neglecting your greenhouse up to this point, it might just be a culmination of dust. But if due diligence was applied, this might indicate a spider mite infestation. Spider mites will leave spotting and yellowing on foliage in their wake.

Pest control actions

Mite activities are enhanced by hot, dry conditions. Therefore regular weeding is required to eliminate and prevent infestations. Mites can be controlled by deploying a miticide in broad form. Identifying the type of mite is advisable since there are good and bad mites. Beneficial predatory mites consume the pilfering mites, so a broad-spectrum miticide will kill the good ones and cause an outbreak of baddies. Mites can be rinsed off the foliage and are effective upon regular application, together with neem oil or other horticultural sprays since they are non-toxic.

Whiteflies

These bugs are identified by their wings and soft bodies. They closely resemble mealybugs and aphids. Even though they are winged, they aren't classified as flies but can fly. Whiteflies are triangular and 1/12 inches in diameter. They are typically found in clusters on the bottom of the foliage. Lastly, they are also diurnal in nature. You can spot them easily at night since they scatter when disturbed.

Plant damages caused

Whiteflies also make use of mouthparts that suck and feed on plant liquids.

Signs of infestation

A whitefly infestation can be seen during heavy feeding times when the crops will weaken and render them unable to perform photosynthesis. The foliage will wilt, turn yellow or pale, and grow slowly. Sometimes, the foliage can be seen shriveling and falling off the crops.

Pest control actions

The first line of defense will always be regularly inspecting your plants. When this tactic is deployed, start by blasting them with a spray of water from a bottle or a hose. Furthermore, crops can be sprayed during the nighttime with a solution of water and insecticidal soap. A solution of dish soap and water works equally well. Should the infestation recur and at wit's end, you can also use a handheld vacuum.

Author's Top Tip

Always empty the vacuum after use before storing it away.

CHAPTER 22:
COMMON PLANT DISEASES AND CONTROLLING THEM

Plant diseases are states of local or systemic abnormally physiological plant functionings. This results from prolonged and continual irritation from biotic or infectious disease agents also called phytopathogenic organisms.

Although many greenhouse plant diseases exist, they can be categorized into three main categories:

- bacterial
- fungal
- viral

We'll now look at these three categories in more detail.

Bacterial

When it comes to plant-based bacterial diseases, they are caused by six different types of genera. The types are:

- Xanthomonas
- Streptomyces
- Pseudomonas
- Corynebacterium
- Agrobacterium

Blight

When 'blight' is mentioned in a room with greenhouse gardeners, you'll most likely hear groans or grumbles of frustration. This is a common bacterial plant disease. Its destruction is severe. For example, when it hits a patch of tomatoes, it destroys the crop by attacking and killing the plant's fruits, foliage, and stems. If left untreated, it can be disastrous. Luckily, as swiftly as it sets in, it can be controlled just as swiftly.

Cause

Most types of blight result from fungal or bacterial infestations. These infestations assault plant roots and other quick plant tissues. Both of these infestations predominantly occur during moist and cool conditions. Commercial plant favorites such as apples, potatoes, and tomatoes are especially predisposed.

Spread

Blight proliferates via fungal spores that are transferred by elements such as animals, insects, water, and wind that they, in turn, pick up from infected crops, which they then drop on the soil.

Diagnosis

Early and Late blight are two different types of this bacterial plant disease. They manifest when the first true fruits appear on tomatoes. It starts showing in the form of minute brown lesions on the bottom foliage. These lesions grow and resemble rings that look like a shooting target and produce dead plant tissue at the 'bullseye.' The tissue on the outer ring becomes yellow and later brown before dying and dropping to the ground.

Early blight doesn't directly harm fruits, but the resulting loss of protective leaves will end up causing fruit damage due to direct sunlight. This condition is called sun scald.

Late blight, on the other hand, affects tomato plants at any time of their growth cycle. Signs start manifesting through damaged and dark plant tissue on the edge of the tomato foliage. This damage then spreads via the foliage, all the way to the plant stem.

All types of early blight can survive the cold winter temperatures by remaining dormant in the soil. As soon as the temperatures soar, the disease returns. Conversely, late blight types can't survive in cold climates as it needs live tissue to grow. But factors such as a strong gust of wind can deposit spores 30 miles further.

Cure

Adequate blight control and prevention includes destroying the infected plant anatomy. This can be achieved by using blight-resistant varieties or seeds free from diseases during sowing. Furthermore, crop rotation, pruning and trimming, and plant spacing can improve air circulation and prevent pest carriers from transmitting diseases between plants. Lastly, antibiotics and fungicides help combat blight too.

Other severe types of bacterial plant diseases include powdery mildew and root rot.

Fungal

This type of fungal disease is diverse and tends to affect all plant parts. The affected plant part anatomy includes:

- crown
- seeds
- sheath
- spikes

There are four main types of fungal plant diseases:

- necrosis
- soft rot
- tumors
- wilt

Wilt

Wilt is a common plant disease resulting from water loss in the foliage and stems of crops. Plants affected by this disease lose their pomposity and then bend and droop.

Cause

Wilt can manifest from waterlogged soil or drought conditions. Crops wilt when they can't send the needed moisture to leaves and stems. However, when wilt occurs over short periods, no harm is caused. It's entirely natural for wilt to appear on plants on hot days. This is because moisture evaporates faster from the leaves than the roots can consume.

Spread

Fungal infestations are spread by elements such as clothing, contaminated working equipment, infected crop cuttings, soil, wind, and water.

Diagnosis

Accurately identifying wilt will go a long way in deploying the best prevention and control methods. Some symptoms may include lower leaf-yellowing, shriveling stems and stunted growth, and discoloration in vascular regions. It's also known that affected crops might curl on one side of the plant foliage.

Cure

Each symptom will have its own cure. So it's vital to target the actual problem at hand. For example, all pruning shears should be sterilized, disease-resistant varieties should be planted, and lastly, biological fungicides can be applied.

Viral

Viral diseases are pathogenic particles in the plant insides that infest the crop's living organs. In this book, we'll look at the Tobacco Mosaic disease variant.

Tobacco Mosaic

This virus, also known as TMV, spreads very quickly between two plants. It's a common crop disease that affects plants worldwide.

Cause and Spread

There are a variety of causes of the Tobacco Mosaic disease. Some include smokers smoking cigarettes, containing the disease, which is spread from their hands to healthy plants. In addition, critters are not exempted from transmission since chewing insects contribute to the spread by munching on infected crops and then transmitting the disease to healthy plants by chewing on them in return.

Diagnosis

The first signs of TMV start to manifest around ten days after the infection has occurred. The crops don't usually die off, but their growth is severely stunted. For instance, in the case of tomatoes, certain Tobacco Mosaic virus strains result in misshapen fruits, different colored tomatoes, and a delay in fruit ripening.

The symptoms that appear will depend on factors such as the type and age of the plant, strain variety, and climate. However, common signs include yellowing, plant tissue necrosis, and dry patches.

Cure

Unfortunately, there's no chemical cure for this disease. The first line of defense is to plant virus-resistant varieties. Next, all infected crops must be removed and destroyed, and tools must be disinfected. Lastly, washing your hands and implementing a strict hygiene regime amongst workers is highly encouraged.

Some other examples of viral plant diseases include Peanut Shunt and Lettuce Mosaic.

Now that we've discussed plant diseases and keeping them at bay let's tackle the actual structure.

CHAPTER 23:
GREENHOUSE CLEANING AND MAINTENANCE

We already know greenhouses are wonderful additions in providing a sustainable food option and the joy of managing your own garden. However, because these systems work so hard, it's only natural that they will need regular cleaning and maintenance.

Greenhouse cleaning refers to the sanitization inside and outside the greenhouse. On the other hand, maintenance involves repairing cracks and replacing broken windows, for example.

So why clean your greenhouse? No matter your greenhouse's material, it will significantly benefit from frequent maintenance and cleaning. In addition, an annual clean-up of sorts is vital in preventing diseases and pests from setting foot inside the application.

No matter which plants you sow, each will require maintenance such as sanitization, preparation, and even removing redundant or infected crops. Therefore, a frequent maintenance schedule will be handy and should be done right throughout the year. I also recommend an annual "spring cleaning" session in the fall to prepare your greenhouse for the following year.

Let's start with how and where to clean your greenhouse.

Greenhouse Maintenance and Cleaning Guide

When you make time to maintain and clean your greenhouse at the end of the growing season, you will save time when spring comes, meaning your energies can be focused elsewhere.

The greatest benefit of all is that you will go into the next growing season knowing that you've done all to ensure a healthy crop yield.

Having said this, let's now look at an example of a greenhouse cleaning and maintenance guide.

Plants

Select a time when the temperature is constantly warm for a few days in a row. Then, clear the greenhouse of all crops (including weeds). Weeds should get special attention since their roots will have been established in the soil by now.

Check your entire structure for signs or symptoms of pests and diseases. This includes checking the plants thoroughly (especially the citrus trees and ornamental tropical plants).

Place any infected crops in a quarantine area until the problem has been safely mitigated.

Containers and Equipment

All greenhouse tools, equipment, pots, and containers must be cleaned and sterilized with a soapy water and bleach solution. I recommend using about ¾ cup of oxygenated bleach to one gallon of water.

Check your pot and seed tray stock and check which containers can be reused or must be thrown away. Then, wash the containers and keep them away from the greenhouse for the time being.

Soil

Dispose of any 'old' soil in your greenhouse. Then, add it to the compost heap for a year to rejuvenate and resurrect, which can be used in the structure again. It's important to cycle the soil in this manner, since stale soil can contain harmful pathogens such as grubs and root aphids.

The stale soil from the last growing season should be replaced with fresh soil that is disease-free and only from a reputable brand. This should be done in the spring or before the new plants are sown. Remember to tackle the soil in the containers, plant beds, under benches, and between paths.

Sweep and rake your greenhouse and treat the entire inside structure with a dusting of diatomaceous earth before leaving your greenhouse dormant until the next growing season.

Irrigation Systems

All holding tanks and irrigation lines should be cleaned from algae and pests like gnats. If left untreated, it threatens crop root systems. I recommend using a solution of ¾ oxygenated bleach to a gallon of hot water. Use this to scrub the reservoirs, holding tanks, dripper heads, and even the irrigation lines.

Greenhouse Structure

Overwintering pests love to seek refuge inside a greenhouse. Unfortunately, wood is the worst material to harbor insects like whiteflies and thrips, while metal-framed greenhouses pose the least risk (but still require sanitization).

The best action to take is to use the oxygenated bleach and water mixture I mentioned earlier and wash the entire internal and external greenhouse with this solution. Next, if your greenhouse boasts any wooden features, apply a helping of horticultural oil (veggie-based) to all wooden areas. I recommend using a brush for this task since it will allow for seepage into hard-to-reach places, and will suffocate the harmful bugs in hiding.

Next, allowing your greenhouse to remain empty and dormant for as long as possible is crucial. Once the time comes, remember to add fresh soil to the greenhouse and introduce disease-resistant or disease-free seeds.

Continual Maintenance and Cleaning Tips

Some additional tips and tricks I'd like to share with you include:

- Avoiding the overlapping and intercropping of plants to reduce the transmission of diseases to healthy crops.
- Attend to all weeds as soon as possible as they can harbor a host of diseases, which can be passed between plants.

- Remove infected plants out of the greenhouse as soon as they are diagnosed. This way, the cleanup will be less time-consuming, and more importantly, the spread will be instantly controlled.

- Ensure strict hygiene and sanitation measures are put in place. This includes washing hands, sterilizing all tools, and wearing shoe protectors.

Repairs

There are a range of potential repair jobs you always need to monitor inside your greenhouse. This includes putting loose glazing clips in place and securing it with a silicone-based sealant. This will supply additional wind protection.

All broken, chipped, or cracked glass and polycarbonate should be fixed or replaced as soon as possible. In case of an emergency, plastic-covered cardboard sheets can be used and secured with glazing tape.

Any tears in plastic sheeting can be fixed by securing them with glazing tape. Squares of polyethylene can be used to repair large holes and are also secured with glazing tape.

However, as mentioned earlier, ensure that replacement takes place as soon as possible to avoid losses.

Weed Control

Your first line of defense in preventing the development of weeds is to sanitize your greenhouse regularly as part of a maintenance regime. Weeds can be controlled by using fresh growing mediums and keeping the external greenhouse clean and weed-free.

It will also help to regularly mow around the greenhouse, as this will discourage the growth of weeds. Weeds should be removed as soon as they are noticed to decrease the change of flowering and seed production.

Physical barriers such as weed block fabrics can be used as they discourage the establishment of weed roots on greenhouse foundations. I recommend leaving the material uncovered to allow easy sweeping. Any tears in the fabric or worn spots should be replaced and repaired quickly to avoid weed germination.

Existing weeds should be removed by hand or using relevant herbicides. Postemergence pesticides are the best solution in this case. Smaller seedlings can be treated with contact herbicides.

Part Two Summary: Greenhouse Gardening Tips and Tricks

If you're lucky enough to have a greenhouse, then you know it's a great way to extend the growing season and get a jump start on the gardening year. But even if you don't have a greenhouse, these tips and tricks will help you get the most out of your garden.

Start With a Clean Slate

Before you start planting, make sure to give your greenhouse a good cleaning. This will help ensure your plants are healthy and free of pests and diseases.

Get Organized

Create a planting schedule and stick to it. This will help you stay on top of watering, fertilizing, and other care tasks.

Ventilate

Make sure to open the vents or doors of your greenhouse on warm days. This will help prevent overheating and provide much-needed ventilation for your plants.

Protect Your Plants From Pests

One of the best things about a greenhouse is that it can protect your plants from pests and diseases. However, it's still important to be proactive about pest control. Inspect your plants regularly and take action if you see any pests or diseases.

Keep an Eye on the Weather

If a cold snap is forecasted, take steps to protect your plants. Cover them with blankets or tarps, and consider bringing them inside if possible.

Make the most of the space

If you're tight on space, consider growing vertically. For example, hang plants from the ceiling or walls, or invest in a rolling rack to maximize floor space.

Keep it clean

Maintaining good hygiene is essential for both you and your plants. Wash your hands before and after working in the greenhouse, and disinfect surfaces regularly.

Have fun!

Gardening should be enjoyable, so make sure to take some time to relax and enjoy your greenhouse. Watch your plants grow, experiment with new varieties, and savor the fruits (and vegetables!) of your labor.

BONUS CHAPTER:
TEN GREENHOUSE PLANS

Introduction to DIY Greenhouse Plans

As promised, here is the much-awaited bonus chapter I mentioned earlier in the book. This will give you some visual insight into the type of greenhouses you can build and what they look like.

Disclaimer: Please note that these are not extremely detailed instructions on building a greenhouse. In fact, you would need a book per greenhouse plan in order to achieve the desired result. Instead, these plans will give you an indication and provide inspiration on which layouts you can consider for your first greenhouse, based on the factors covered in an earlier chapter in the book. I've also not included the dimensions since this is part of customization and will be entirely at your discretion.

Rather, I am providing some illustrations of greenhouse plans for beginners. You can refer to the first section of the book for more details.

With that being said, I will provide some illustrations of greenhouse plans for beginners. Feel free to refer to Part One of the book for a detailed description, including pros and cons. I've also ranked them in difficulty from 1-10, with 10 being the most difficult to build.

Greenhouse Kits

Aluminum Frame Rectangular Greenhouse Kits

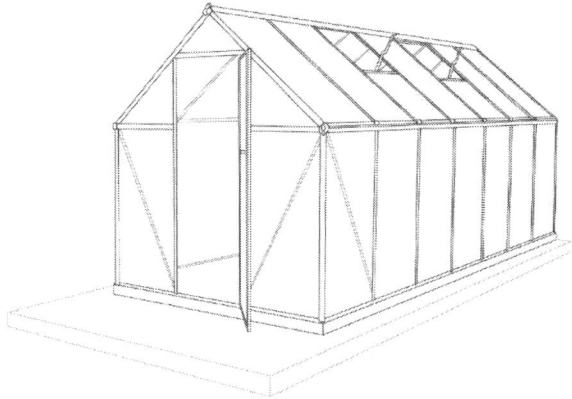

This is a greenhouse kit that we've discussed in detail in Part One of the book and is one of the most simple to create.

Difficulty Level: 1/10

Cost: $ 220.00–$ 250.00 for a typical 8 inch by 16 inch structure.

Time to construct: Two to three days on average.

Recommended use: This kit is the best option for almost any plant. The internal layout is highly customizable. It is recommended as a first greenhouse project for beginners that want to test various plants and sense what they would like to use a greenhouse for.

Stylish Hexagonal Greenhouse Kits

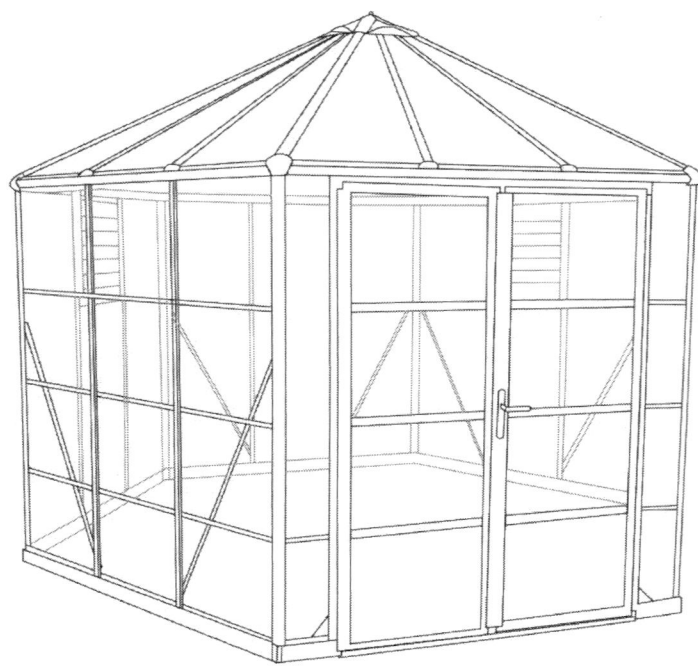

This is a more stylish and more expensive greenhouse kit if compared with the previous one. You usually find Hexagonal greenhouse kits of various width – the most typical kits are 8' or 12' wide.

Difficulty Level: 2/10

Cost: $ 1,490.00–$ 2 ,000.00 for a 45-square foot structure.

Time to construct: Approximately eight hours.

Recommended use: Hanging plants and for growing crops in containers. This greenhouse can house many shelves. It is also a good kit for growing flowers as they can get sun exposition from all the directions.

Season-Extender Portable Greenhouse Kits

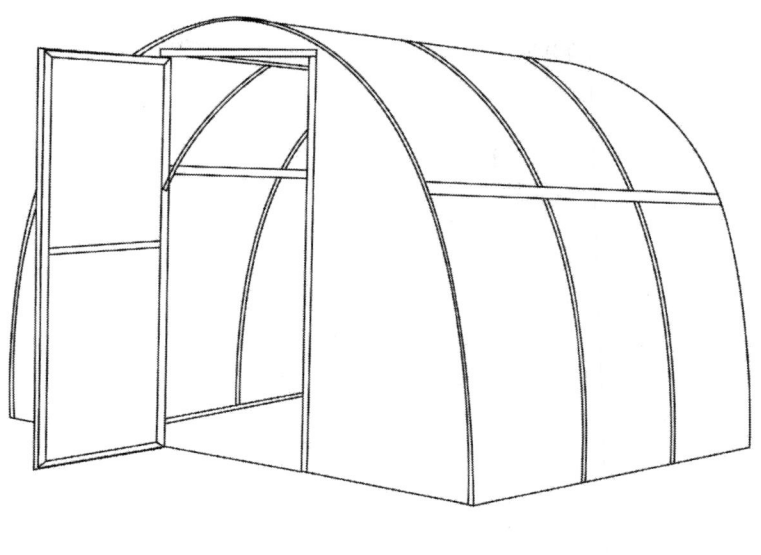

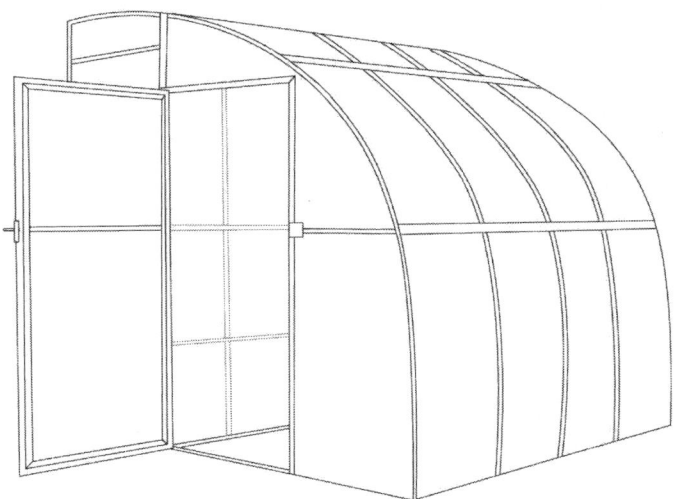

2 versions of this kit are usually available: "complete arch" and "lean-to". Such kits are usually put "over plants". It is in fact a portable option.

Difficulty Level: 3/10

Cost: $34.00–$52.00 for sizes ranging between 2' by 2" and 4' by 3".

Time to construct: As little as two hours.

Recommended use: Used for plants that won't be put in a greenhouse and is portable. Its specific purpose is to extend plant growing seasons by six to eight weeks and even longer in other instances.

Wooden Frame Greenhouses

This is the very first plan for "DIYers" with relative experience in construction. It is still a beginner-friendly plan. If you want the greenhouse to be a permanent construction, you can consider different types of foundatons. On the other hand, if you are planning a mobile model, just prepare a rectangular frame. In both cases, however, you need to prepare the area where you want to build the greenhouse to ensure that it is perfectly leveled.

You will need to secure wooden posts to the base frame with screws followed by the head frame. Then you build the roof and install the door.

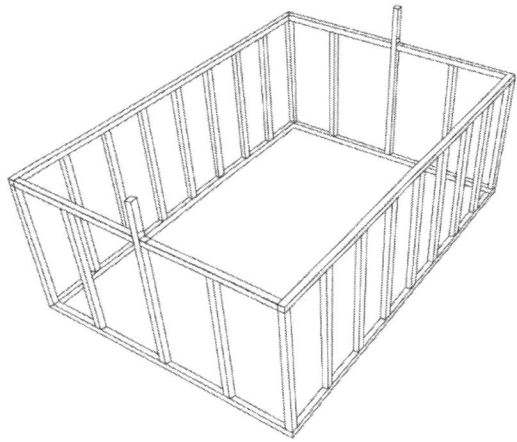

Once you have built the frame of the greenhouse, you have to install either polycarbonate panels or plastic foil on the outside of the greenhouse. In case you opt for plastic foil, make sure that you apply plastic strips to support the foil.

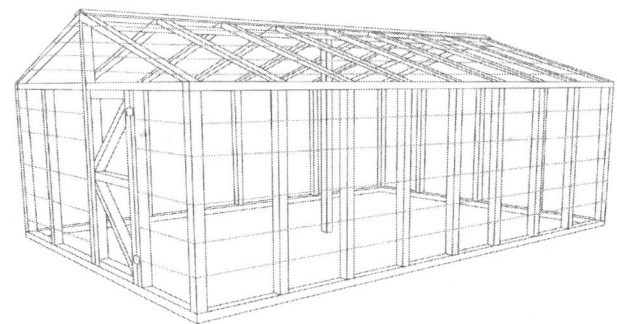

If you don't have enough construction experience you can also consider hiring a contractor. It is not a difficult job and it should not be too expensive. A contractor can usually build a similar structure in a few hours.

Difficulty Level: 6/10

Cost: $1.00 per linear foot.

Time to construct: Depending on the size and on your level of construction experience, but anything from a few hours to a few days or weeks.

Recommended use: Multi-use that includes herbs, flowers, fruit and veggies.

Simple Hoop Houses/Polytunnels

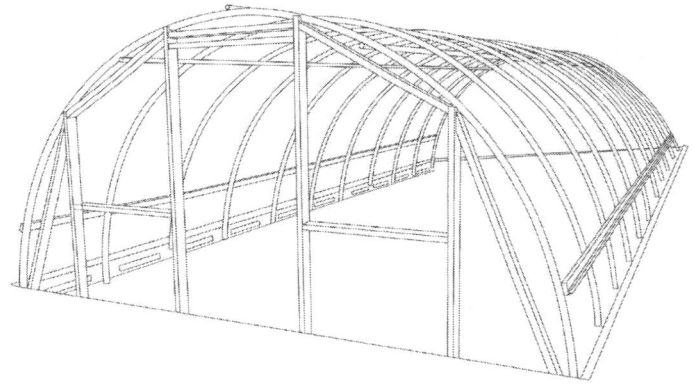

I have already described earlier in the book the reasons for building a hoop house over other options.

You can plan the dimensions of your hoop house based on your needs: which plants are you planning to grow? Are you building in an area with strong wind or heavy snowfalls? Do you have a tvery limited budget?

A hoop house is a simple structure usually constructed with a foundation made of pressure-treated wooden posts, with PVC bows. Plastic foil is added to cover the structure.

Even for this plan, if you have no experience in construction, you can consider hiring a contractor. However, a beginner-friendly hoop house can easily be built also by a complete beginner.

Once you have built the foundation, start to place the PVC bows. In addition, add purlins perpendicular to the bows. Finally, the plastic foil is attached to the foundation. Additional wooden posts can be added on top of the PVC bows and the film is added to the posts.

In case you live in an area with heavy snowfall or strong winds, you can consider adding braces to support the bows.

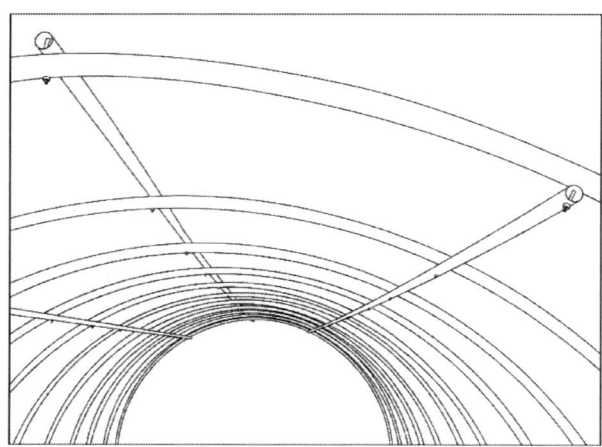 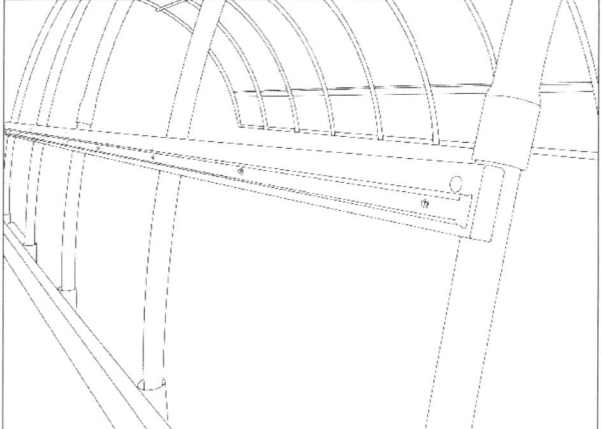

The process above should give you a simple and general overview of the steps that you should follow to build your hoop house. The process can, of course, vary according to the additional features that you decide to install and also your level of construction experience.

Difficulty Level: 7/10

Cost: Between $5.00–$10.00 per square foot.

Time to construct: Depending on the size, but anything from a few hours to a few days or weeks.

Recommended use: Multi-use that includes herbs, flowers, fruit and veggies.

Dome Greenhouses

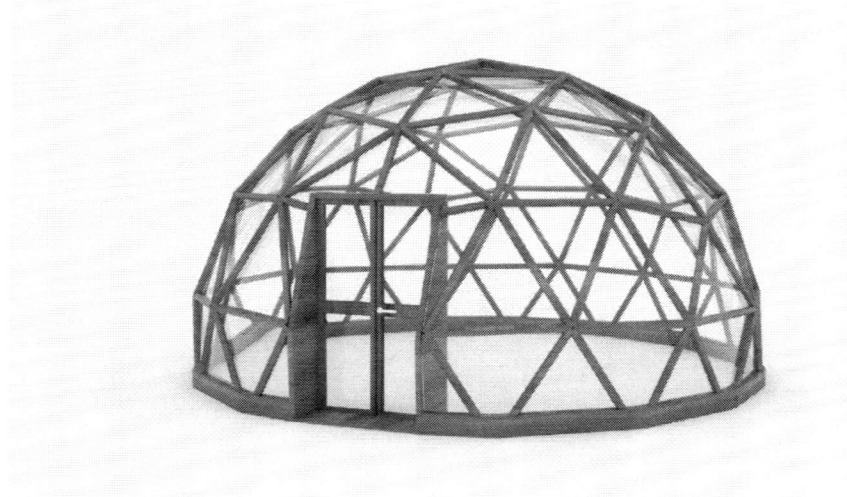

This is the optimal greenhouse if you live in an environment with heavy snowfalls, strong winds, and little light – remember igloos?

Usually, dome greenhouses are built without foundations. In case you want to build a more stable greenhouse, you can also consider foundations: it depends on your needs and requirements in terms of portability.

Like the other beginner-friendly plans covered in this book, the materials required are few and easy to source. You will just need wooden posts, screws, automatic window opener hinges for the door and the windows. Finally, plastic foil or polycarbonate panels are required for the cover.

To calculate the dimensions of your greenhouse you can use one of the many Geodome calculators that are available online. Just search online for a Geodome calculator and you will have plenty of choices. You will need to choose the geodesic frequency. My advice is to consider frequencies from 2V to 4V. A smaller plan can consider lower frequencies. I don't recommend choosing frequencies that are higher than 4V. When you plan your dimensions, keep in mind that the height will always be half of the width of the greenhouse.

As a first step, you need to prepare the wooden beams. It is crucial that you cut them at a precise angle. This precision is crucial as you will need to attach the beams together and you cannot have any gauge if you want a structure that is as stable as possible. Therefore, when you cut the beams, ensure that you are using a high-precision tool, such as a radial arm saw. Geodome calculators can precisely define the angle you need.

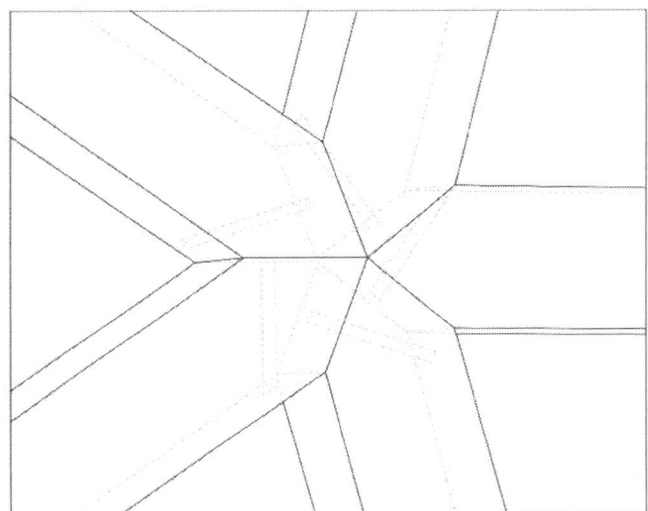 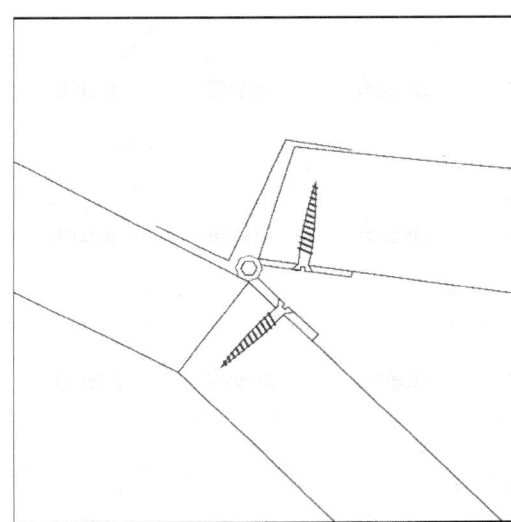

You can now start to assemble the wooden beams and secure them with screws. While assembling them, you also need to keep in mind that you need to plan space for a door and windows. If you are not planning to install a cooling system, decide on the right amount of windows to keep the temperature that you require for growing your plants.

Finally, you will need to apply the cover - plastic foil or polycarbonate panels. You can again use a geodome calculator to obtain the exact size of the panels.

Difficulty Level: 7/10

Cost: $9,950.00–$22,650.00 Price ranges in sizes from 15" to 26".

Time to construct: Depending on the size, but anything from a few hours to a few days or weeks.

Recommended use: Multi-use that includes herbs, flowers, fruit, and veggies.

Cold Frames

Cold frames are an easy option when it comes to greenhouse plans. They are easy to build, compact, low-maintenance, and can be moved easily.

The steps for building a DIY cold frame are a bit different from the processes described for the other plans. Your project should start with the decision on what lid you want to use for your cold frame. You can use plastic foil, other transparent materials such as polycarbonate sheets, or you can use an old window. In case you decide to use a window, the dimensions of your cold frame will be tied to the dimensions of the window.

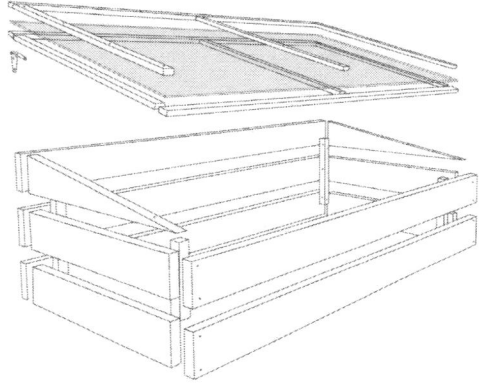

Even for this project, you will only need a few materials: wooden beams, wood screws, a couple of hinges to attach the lid to the frame, and your lid.

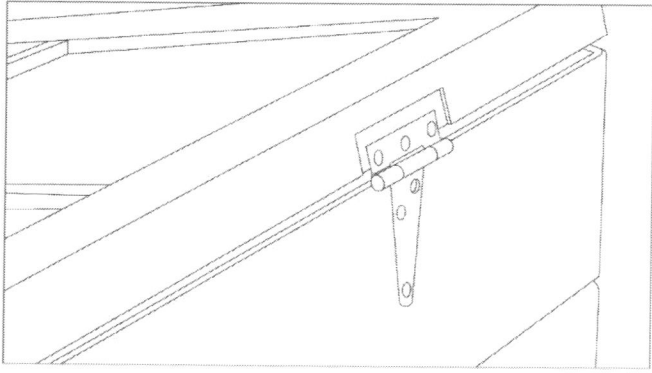

For building the frame you will use pressure-treated wooden beams, with dimensions matching the dimensions of the lid. Note that the back of the frame is one beam higher than the front. This generates a slope for good drainage and maximum sunlight exposure. For the sides of the cold frame you will need to cut one beam in half diagonally to match the slope. Then you can screw all of the boards to put the frame together.

Once you have prepared the frame and the lid, you can now attach them through the hinges.

A cold frame can be very warm during the summer. To keep the right level of ventilation, you can use a piece of wood to keep the cold frame open when the sun is stronger.

Difficulty Level: 2/10

Cost: $30.00–$150.00 depending on the desired size.

Time to construct: Building a cold-frame usually takes few hours, maximum 1 day.

Recommended use: Multi-use that includes herbs, flowers, fruit, and veggies.

Greenhouses From Old Windows

As a first step, you should look around and try to get as many old windows as you can. If possible, try to get 2 pairs of the same type of window, so that you can use one for each side of your greenhouse. Collecting windows by pair makes the shaping of the frame part much easier.

Once you have retrieved enough windows, you can start to combine them and define the layout of the side walls of your greenhouse. Holes are not a problem, you can fill them with some wood or cover them with plastic film or layers.

You now need to shape a frame (I suggest using wooden beams) to hold the windows. The frame will hold the weight of the windows and will define the shape of the greenhouse. Remember to save some space for the door and for eventual fans, if you plan o install any.

Once you have built the frames for the four sides, you can now erect them and give shape to your greenhouse. During this step, you can also consider building foundations, based on your mobility requirements. You can now place the windows on the frame, by using some screws.

You cannot use windows for the roof: they are too heavy. You can consider using lighter waterproof material such as plastic film or polycarbonate panels.

Difficulty Level: 7/10

Cost: $300.00 for a small to medium-sized greenhouse.

Time to construct: Depending on the size, but anything from a few hours to a few days or weeks.

Recommended use: Multi-use that includes herbs, flowers, fruit, and veggies.

Lean-To Greenhouses

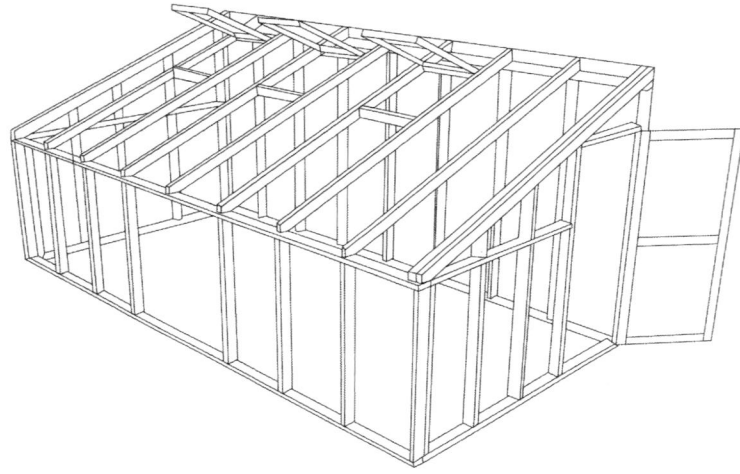

The process to build this plan is exactly the same as the process that I have described for the wooden frame greenhouse. The only difference is that this is the lean-to version.

Difficulty Level: 6/10

Cost: $10.00–$25.00 per square foot.

Time to construct: Depending on the size, but anything from a few hours to a few days or weeks.

Recommended use: Multi-use that includes herbs, flowers, fruit, and veggies.

CONCLUSION

We might think that we are nurturing our garden, but of course, it's our garden that is really nurturing us.
—Jenny Uglow

The Benefits...reiterated!

Greenhouse gardening has many benefits that make it an excellent option for those looking to get started in gardening or to expand their current operation. One of the biggest advantages of greenhouse gardening is the controlled environment that it offers. By growing in a greenhouse, you can maintain consistent temperatures and humidity levels, which can be challenging to do outdoors. In addition, this makes it easier to grow delicate plants that might not survive in harsh conditions.

Another benefit of greenhouse gardening is the extended growing season that it offers. In most parts of the country, the outdoor growing season is limited by cold weather. But in a greenhouse, you can extend your growing season by starting plants early in the spring and continuing to grow them into the fall and even winter. This means you can enjoy fresh, homegrown fruits and vegetables year-round.

Finally, greenhouse gardening can save you money in the long run. Because you can control the environment inside a greenhouse, you can reduce your reliance on expensive inputs like heat lamps and artificial fertilizers. This means that your overall gardening costs will be lower in the long run.

So if you're looking for a way to get started in gardening or expand your current operation, consider greenhouse gardening. It offers many benefits that make it a great option for those looking to get the most out of their garden.

Where and How to Learn More About Greenhouse Gardening

If you're interested in learning more about greenhouse gardening, there are a few resources that can be helpful. Many nurseries and garden centers will have books on the subject, which can be a great way to get started. You can also find some good information online, including on websites devoted to greenhouse gardening. Forums can also be a valuable resource, as you can connect with other greenhouse gardeners and get advice and tips from them. Finally, don't forget to ask your friends or family members who might have experience with this type of gardening. They may be able to offer some helpful insights.

Greenhouse Gardening as a Business

If you're thinking about starting a greenhouse gardening business, there are a few things you should know. First, it's essential to have a passion for plants and gardening. Greenhouse gardening can be a very rewarding business, but it takes hard work and dedication to make it successful.

Second, you'll need to invest in quality equipment and materials. For example, a good greenhouse will cost you several thousand dollars, and you'll also need to purchase grow lights, fans, soil, and other supplies.

Third, you'll need to create a market for your plants. There are many ways to do this, including selling at farmers' markets or setting up a website or online store. You'll need to put in some time and effort to promote your business and get customers.

Fourth, you'll need to be prepared for the challenges of running a business. Greenhouse gardening can be unpredictable, and you may have slow seasons where you don't make much money. You'll need to be prepared for these ups and downs and have a plan for how you'll keep your business afloat during tough times.

If you're ready to take on the challenge of starting a greenhouse gardening business, there's no time like the present! Just remember to do your research, invest in quality supplies, create a market for your plants, and be prepared for the ups and downs of running a business. With hard work and dedication, you can make your greenhouse gardening business a success!

Some Greenhouse Mistakes to Avoid

No matter how much you may want to grow your own plants and vegetables, there are some greenhouse mistakes that you should avoid. Otherwise, you could end up with a lot of problems down the road. Here are four big mistakes to avoid when it comes to greenhouses:

- **Not Ventilating Properly:** One of the most critical functions of a greenhouse is to trap heat inside, but that doesn't mean that you shouldn't ventilate at all. If your greenhouse gets too hot, your plants will start to suffer. Make sure you have some sort of ventilation system in place so that the air can circulate and the temperature can stay regulated.

- **Not Heating Properly:** Just as important as ventilation is heating. If it gets too cold in your greenhouse, your plants will die. Make sure you have an efficient heating system in place so that your plants can stay warm and toasty all winter long.

- **Not Watering Properly:** Water is essential for plant growth, so make sure you're giving your plants enough water. However, you don't want to overwater them. Too much water can actually drown your plants. Make sure you're watering on a regular basis and keeping an eye on the moisture levels in the soil.

- **Not Fertilizing Properly:** Plants need nutrients to grow, so ensure you're fertilizing them regularly. However, you don't want to overdo it. Too much fertilizer can actually burn your plants. Stick to a regular fertilizing schedule, and don't go overboard.

If you avoid these four big mistakes, you'll be well on your way to successful greenhouse gardening. Just make sure you do your research and take the time to set up your greenhouse properly. It'll be well worth it in the end!

I genuinely hope you enjoyed reading this book as much as I've written it. And my deepest hope is that it was packed with all the information to guide and encourage you on *your* greenhouse gardening adventure.

In exchange for feedback regarding this book, and what you'd like me to cover in the next book, please send me an email at michael.york68@yahoo.com, and I will happily share a free high-quality greenhouse sowing calendar, which you can download, print, and use in your own greenhouse.

Thank you for selecting and for reading my book. I hope it has given you the inspiration and passion to start your own greenhouse designs.

I would appreciate it if you would take the time to write a positive review on **Amazon**.

Until next time, enjoy your gardening endeavors!

REFERENCES

Abadalla, D. A. (1967, February 23). *Growing blueberries from seed.* Cooperative Extension: Maine Wild Blueberries - University of Maine Cooperative Extension. https://extension.umaine.edu/blueberries/factsheets/cultivated-lowbush-blueberries/growing-blueberries-from-seed/ admin. (2015, March 6). *Boom irrigation systems.* Center for Agriculture, Food, and the Environment. https://ag.umass.edu/greenhouse-floriculture/fact-sheets/boom-irrigation-systems

Aladin. (n.d.). *Voila, Romania - August weather forecast and climate information.* Weather Atlas. https://www.weather-atlas.com/en/romania/voila-weather-august

Alfaro, D. (2020, August 23). *Curious about chives? Here's what you need to know.* The Spruce. https://www.thespruceeats.com/what-are-chives-995617

Alice. (2020, June 23). *How to build a budget greenhouse (and what to put in it first!).* Our Daily Homestead. https://ourdailyhomestead.com/how-to-build-a-budget-greenhouse/#what-does-a-greenhouse-usually-cost

AMERICAN PEST PROFESSIONALS. (2019, May 22). *4 benefits of bees (and what to do about their disadvantages).* https://www.americanpestpros.com/4-benefits-of-bees-and-what-to-do-about-their-disadvantages

Aphids. (n.d.). Old Farmer's Almanac. https://www.almanac.com/pest/aphids#

Artificial pollination. (2019, March 21). BYJU'S. https://byjus.com/biology/artificial-pollination/

Ashwanden, C. (2016, November 28). *Walipini greenhouses – Some DIY tips.* THE PERMACULTURE RESEARCH INSTITUTE. https://www.permaculturenews.org/2016/11/28/walipini-greenhouses-diy-tips/

Bacterial diseases of plants - An overview. (n.d.). ScienceDirect. https://www.sciencedirect.com/topics/agricultural-and-biological-sciences/bacterial-diseases-of-plants

Badget, B. (2022, February 25). *How to grow chives indoors.* Gardening KNOW HOW. https://www.gardeningknowhow.com/edible/herbs/chives/growing-chives-indoors.htm

Baessler, L. (2019, July 12). *Raspberry fertilizing needs – When to feed raspberries.* Gardening KNOW HOW. https://www.gardeningknowhow.com/edible/fruits/raspberry/when-to-feed-raspberries.htm

Baessler, L. (2020, July 18). *Feeding seedlings: Should I fertilize seedlings?* Gardening KNOW HOW. https://www.gardeningknowhow.com/garden-how-to/soil-fertilizers/should-you-fertilize-seedlings

Bartok, J. (2019, March 26). *10 tips for keeping your greenhouse cool this summer.* Greenhouse MANAGEMENT. https://www.greenhousemag.com/article/tech-solutions-10-tips-for-keeping-your-greenhouse-cool-this-summer/

Bartok, John. W. (2019, February 28). *The advantages of subirrigation.* Greenhouse MANAGEMENT. https://www.greenhousemag.com/article/tech-solutions-advantages-subirrigation/

BBC Gardeners World Magazine. (2020, June 30). *The best planters and containers for strawberries.* BBC Gardeners World Magazine. https://www.gardenersworld.com/plants/the-best-containers-for-strawberries/

Bethke, J. A., & Dreistadt, S. H. (2001). *Fungus Gnats management guidelines.* Statewide Integration Pest Management Progam. http://ipm.ucanr.edu/PMG/PESTNOTES/pn7448.html

Blight | Definition, description, examples, & treatment. (n.d.). Encyclopedia Britannica. https://www.britannica.com/science/blight

Blueberry | Diseases and pests, description, uses, propagation. (n.d.). PlantVillage. https://plantvillage.psu.edu/topics/blueberry/infos#

Bob, & Margaret. (n.d.). *Bob's projects & ideas: A-Frame greenhouse.* Northern Greenhouse. https://www.northerngreenhouse.com/projects-and-ideas/bobs-projects-and-ideas/a-frame-greenhouse.shtml

Boeckmann, C. (2019, March 31). *Strawberries.* Old Farmer's Almanac. https://www.almanac.com/plant/strawberries

Boyette, M., Wilson, L. G., & Estes, E. (1989, July 1). *Postharvest cooling and handling of strawberries.* NC State Extension Publications. https://content.ces.ncsu.edu/postharvest-cooling-and-handling-of-strawberries

Butler, C. D. (2018a, October 11). *Planting and growing California Poppy (Eschscholzia california).* GARDENZEUS. https://www.gardenzeus.com/planting-and-growing-california-poppy-eschscholzia-california/

Butler, C. D. (2018b, October 15). *California Poppy: Tips and precautions for care and watering.* GARDENZEUS. https://www.gardenzeus.com/california-poppy-tips-and-precautions-for-care-and-watering/

Butler, C. D. (2018c, October 15). *Soil and microclimate tips for California Poppy (Eschscholzia california).* GARDENZEUS. https://www.gardenzeus.com/soil-and-microclimate-tips-for-california-poppy-eschscholzia-california/#:~:text=It%20prefers%20well%2Ddrained%20clay

California Poppy. (n.d.). California Department of Fish and Wildlife. https://wildlife.ca.gov/Conservation/Plants/California-Poppy#:~:text=On%20March%202%2C%201903%20the

California Poppy - Flower seed |. (n.d.). Johnny's Selected Seeds. https://www.johnnyseeds.com/flowers/poppy/california-poppy-flower-seed-1229.html?cgid=poppy#start=1

Charbonneau, J. (2019, October 8). *3 reasons to transplant lettuce.* Southern Exposure Seed Exchange. https://blog.southernexposure.com/2019/10/3-reasons-to-transplant-lettuce/

Charles-Lucien Bonaparte, Prince di Canino e di Musignano | French scientist. (n.d.). Encyclopedia Britannica. https://www.britannica.com/biography/Charles-Lucien-Bonaparte-principe-di-Canimo-e-di-Muignano

Chassouant, C. (2019, September 26). *Intensive blueberries production using plastic greenhouses.* HORTI GENERATION. https://horti-generation.com/intensive-blueberries-production-using-plastic-greenhouses/

Chiras, D. (2020a). *The Chinese Greenhouse: Design and Build a Low-Cost, Passive Solar Greenhouse.* New Society Publishers. https://www.amazon.com/Chinese-Greenhouse-Design-Low-Cost-Passive/dp/0865719292/ref=sr_1_1?crid=3MCJTROY0NGN3&keywords=The+Chinese+Greenhouse%3A+Design+and+Build+a+Low-Cost%2C+Passive+Solar+Greenhouse&qid=1646471336&s=books&sprefix=the+chinese+greenhouse+design+and+build+a+low-cost%2C+passive+solar+greenhouse%2Cstripbooks-intl-ship%2C326&sr=1-1

Chiras, D. (2020b, December 9). *Fighting a gardener's wintertime blues with my Chinese Greenhouse.* New Society Publishers. https://newsociety.com/blogs/news/fighting-a-gardeners-wintertime-blues-with-my-chinese-greenhouse

Chives | Diseases and pests, description, uses, propagation. (2010). PlantVillage. https://plantvillage.psu.edu/topics/chives/infos

Choosing a greenhouse type - Our top 8 options. (2019, August 14). INDOOR GARDENING. https://indoorgardening.com/choosing-a-greenhouse-type-8-options/

Choosing the right greenhouse irrigation system. (2020, March 30). Berger. https://www.berger.ca/en/grower-resources/hints-and-tips/choosing-the-right-greenhouse-irrigation-system/

Commercial greenhouse- What is it? (n.d.). Global PLASTIC SHEETING. https://www.globalplasticsheeting.com/commercial-greenhouse-what-is-it

Considerations for subsurface drip irrigation application in humid and sub-humid areas. (2006, December 15). UGA Cooperative Extension. https://extension.uga.edu/publications/detail.html?number=C903&title=Considerations%20for%20Subsurface%20Drip%20Irrigation%20Application%20in%20Humid%20and%20Sub-humid%20Areas

Cost to build a greenhouse | Greenhouse installation cost. (2021, January 5). FIXr. https://www.fixr.com/costs/build-greenhouse

Country Living Magazine. (n.d.). *Absolutely beautiful quotes about summer | Garden quotes, gardening memes, garden inspiration.* Pinterest. https://za.pinterest.com/pin/absolutely-beautiful-quotes-about-summer--198299189821753965/

Cucumbers. (2019, June 11). Old Farmer's Almanac. https://www.almanac.com/plant/cucumbers

Dawe, J. (2018, October 10). *Greenhouse cleaning and maintenance for beginners.* Eartheasy Guides & Articles. https://learn.eartheasy.com/articles/greenhouse-cleaning-and-maintenance-for-beginners/#:~:text=Wash%20your%20entire%20greenhouse%20structure

De Decker, K. (n.d.). *Chinese greenhouses for winter gardening - Organic gardening.* MOTHER EARTH NEWS. https://www.motherearthnews.com/organic-gardening/chinese-greenhouses-for-winter-gardening-zm0z17amzmul

Deckert, T. (2015, January 22). *Modular greenhouses: The next big thing in urban farming?* POP up CITY. https://popupcity.net/observations/modular-greenhouses-the-next-big-thing-in-urban-farming/

Deed, T. (2022, February 22). *Freestanding greenhouses for all plants.* Dengarden. https://dengarden.com/gardening/Freestanding-greenhouse-for-All-Plants

DeMarsay, A. (n.d.). *Growing blueberries in containers.* University of Maryland Extension. https://extension.umd.edu/resource/growing-blueberries-containers

Do Chives Need Full Sun? | Pepper's Home & Garden. (2022, January 20). Pepper's Home & Garden. https://peppershomeandgarden.com/do-chives-need-full-sun/

Doherty, T. (2020, December 8). *What are the greatest risks to your greenhouse in cold climates?* NIP Group. https://nipgroup.com/what-are-the-greatest-risks-to-your-greenhouse-in-cold-climates/

Drake, A. (n.d.). *The essential guide to greenhouse foundations.* In Wisconsin Greenhouse Company. https://wisconsingreenhousecompany.com/wp-content/uploads/2020/04/Wisconsin-Foundation-Guide-Main-1.6.20.pdf

Drip irrigation. (n.d.). NETAFIM. https://www.netafim.co.za/drip-irrigation/

Drip irrigation resource guide. (2022, April 15). Country Farm and Home. https://chathamfarmsupply.com/resources/drip-irrigation-resource-guide

Drip vs. overhead irrigation. (2017, May 17). Senninger. https://www.senninger.com/news/2017/09/27/drip-vs-overhead-irrigation

Dunn, P. (2016, July 18). *Greenhouse management.* Tend Smart Farm. https://www.tend.com/blog/greenhouse-management

Duvauchelle, J. (2018, December 14). *Pest control for Marigolds in a garden.* SFGATE. https://homeguides.sfgate.com/pest-control-marigolds-garden-75515.html

Ellis, M. E. (2021, November 26). *What is a hotbed – Tips for gardening in a hot box.* Gardening KNOW HOW. https://www.gardeningknowhow.com/special/greenhouses/gardening-in-a-hot-box.htm

Emery, M. (2021, January 25). *How to grow cucumbers in a pot.* HGTV. https://www.hgtv.com/outdoors/flowers-and-plants/vegetables/grow-cucumbers-pot

Environmental control systems. (n.d.). University of Arizona. https://cals.arizona.edu/hydroponictomatoes/system.htm

Essential pH management in greenhouse crops: pH and plant nutrition. (2005, March 15). UGA Cooperative Extension. https://extension.uga.edu/publications/detail.html?number=B1256&title=Essential%20pH%20Management%20in%20Greenhouse%20Crops:%20pH%20and%20Plant%20Nutrition

Finley, R. (2022, February 24). *How to build a greenhouse: 8-step DIY greenhouse guide.* MasterClass. https://www.masterclass.com/articles/how-to-build-a-greenhouse#5-materials-you-will-need-to-build-a-greenhouse

Fisher, R. (n.d.). *Top 10 things to do with raspberries.* BBC Goodfood. https://www.bbcgoodfood.com/howto/guide/top-10-things-do-raspberries

Flower Viola. (n.d.). Gardeners Net. https://www.gardenersnet.com/flower/viola.htm

Frizzle Sizzle Yellow-Blue Swirl - Viola seed. (n.d.). Johnny's Selected Seeds. https://www.johnnyseeds.com/flowers/viola-pansy/frizzle-sizzle-yellow-blue-swirl-viola-seed-4453.html?cgid=viola#start=1

Fungal diseases in plants - An overview. (n.d.). ScienceDirect. https://www.sciencedirect.com/topics/agricultural-and-biological-sciences/fungal-diseases-in-plant#:~:text=Fungal%20diseases%20in%20plant%20are

Fusarium Wilt: Symptoms, treatment and control. (n.d.). PLANET NATURAL. https://www.planetnatural.com/pest-problem-solver/plant-disease/fusarium-wilt/

Giant Yellow - Marigold seed. (n.d.). Johnny's Selected Seeds. https://www.johnnyseeds.com/flowers/marigold/giant-yellow-marigold-seed-1884.html?cgid=marigold#start=1

Grant, A. (2021a, May 16). *Can you transplant blueberries: Tips for transplanting blueberry bushes.* Gardening KNOW HOW. https://www.gardeningknowhow.com/edible/fruits/blueberries/transplanting-blueberry-bushes.htm

Grant, A. (2021b, November 2). *Greenhouse location guide: Learn where to put your greenhouse.* Gardening KNOW HOW. https://www.gardeningknowhow.com/special/greenhouses/where-to-put-greenhouse.htm

Grant, A. (2021c, December 15). *Fungus Gnat vs. Shore Fly: How to tell Fungus Gnats and Shore Flies apart.* Gardening KNOW HOW. https://www.gardeningknowhow.com/plant-problems/pests/insects/fungus-gnat-vs-shore-fly.htm

Grant, Bonnie. L. (2020, October 18). *Common Marigold diseases: Learn about diseases in Marigold plants.* Gardening KNOW HOW. https://www.gardeningknowhow.com/ornamental/flowers/marigold/diseases-in-marigold-plants.htm#:~:text=Among%20the%20most%20common%20marigold

Grant, Bonnie. L. (2021, July 5). *Types of mites in garden: Common mites that affect plants.* Gardening KNOW HOW. https://www.gardeningknowhow.com/plant-problems/pests/insects/common-mites-affecting-plants.htm

Greenhouse Emporium. (n.d.). *All greenhouse kits at a glance.* https://greenhouseemporium.com/collections/greenhouse-kits/

Greenhouse facts. (2021, July 19). FACTS Just for KIDS. https://www.factsjustforkids.com/plant-facts/greenhouse-facts-for-kids/

Greenhouse gardening – How to grow cabbage? (2017, July 25). Greenhouse Emporium. https://greenhouseemporium.com/blogs/greenhouse-gardening/greenhouse-gardening-how-to-grow-cabbage/

Greenhouse gardening – How to grow lettuce? (2017, September 13). Greenhouse Emporium. https://greenhouseemporium.com/blogs/greenhouse-gardening/greenhouse-gardening-how-to-grow-lettuce/

Greenhouse irrigation - What's the best watering system? (2021, April 9). Greenhouse Emporium. https://greenhouseemporium.com/blogs/greenhouse-gardening/greenhouse-irrigation-systems/

Greenhouse management: A guide to greenhouse technology and operations. (n.d.). APEX PUBLISHERS. https://www.greenhouse-management.com/greenhouse_management/greenhouse_structures_design/types_greenhouses.htm

Greenhouse management: A guide to operations and technology. (n.d.). APEX PUBLISHERS. https://www.greenhouse-management.com/greenhouse_management/greenhouse_production_systems/capillary_mat_system.htm

Greenhouse planting schedule - A greenhouse planting calendar. (2021, January 24). CERES GREENHOUSE SOLUTIONS. https://ceresgs.com/year-round-greenhouse-planting-calendar/

Greenhouse plants, Ornamental-Fusarium damping-off, wilt, and root rot. (2021, March 26). Pacific Northwest Pest Management Handbooks. https://pnwhandbooks.org/plantdisease/host-disease/greenhouse-plants-ornamental-fusarium-damping-wilt-root-rot#:~:text=The%20fungus%20can%20be%20spread

Greenhouse sprinkler – Overhead watering system for greenhouse. (n.d.). ShinyGrow. https://www.shinygrow.com/products/grenhouse-sprinkler.html

Greenhouse structure types pros & cons. (n.d.). GreenhouseFanatics. https://greenhousefanatics.com/types-greenhouse-structures/

Greenhouse structures. (n.d.). Hytasu Corporation. http://www.hytasu.com/guttercon_greenhouse.htm

Greenhouses: How to choose and where to buy. (2019). Eartheasy. https://learn.eartheasy.com/guides/greenhouses-how-to-choose-and-where-to-buy/

Growing cabbages in containers! (2020, April 30). Balcony Garden Web. https://balconygardenweb.com/how-to-grow-cabbage-in-pots-growing-in-containers/

Growing chives in home gardens. (n.d.). University of Minnesota. https://extension.umn.edu/vegetables/growing-chives

Growing parsley in home gardens. (n.d.). University of Minnesota. https://extension.umn.edu/vegetables/growing-parsley

Gu, M. (n.d.). *High tunnel or greenhouse?* MISSISSIPPI STATE UNIVERSITY. https://extension.msstate.edu/sites/default/files/publications/information-sheets/is1674.pdf

Harness, J. (2020, November 25). *Greenhouse maintenance and repair checklist.* Hunker. https://www.hunker.com/13730205/greenhouse-maintenance-and-repair-checklist

Heber, G. (2020, January 8). *How to grow chives in containers.* Gardener's Path. https://gardenerspath.com/plants/herbs/grow-chives-containers/

Hendry, A. M. (2015, October 29). *How to windproof your greenhouse.* GrowVeg. https://www.growveg.co.za/guides/how-to-windproof-your-greenhouse/

Hicks-Hamblin, K. (2022, February 15). *How to grow tomatoes from seed in 6 easy steps.* GARDENER'S PATH. https://gardenerspath.com/plants/vegetables/grow-tomatoes-seeds-6-easy-steps/

Holt, J. (2018, May 2). *Maximize your strawberry harvest with greenhouse-growing.* Organic Growers School. https://organicgrowersschool.org/maximize-your-strawberry-harvest-with-greenhouse-growing/

Home—Greenhouse kits, commercial & hobby greenhouses, and hydroponic systems. (n.d.). Growers Supply. https://www.growerssupply.com/farm/supplies/home

Horizontal airflow is best for greenhouse air circulation. (2015, March 6). University of Massachusetts Amherst. https://ag.umass.edu/greenhouse-floriculture/fact-sheets/horizontal-air-flow-is-best-for-greenhouse-air-circulation

How greenhouses work: Tips and tricks. (n.d.). Properly Rooted. https://properlyrooted.com/how-does-greenhouse-work/

How much does a commercial greenhouse cost? (2020, June 26). Bosman van Zaal. https://www.bosmanvanzaal.co.za/how-much-does-a-commercial-greenhouse-cost/

How much water do chives need? (2022, April 23). Pepper's Home & Garden. https://peppershomeandgarden.com/how-much-water-chives-need/

How to build a window greenhouse. (1987, November 1). MOTHER EARTH NEWS. https://www.motherearthnews.com/diy/window-greenhouse-zmaz87ndzgoe/

How to choose the best greenhouse. (2020, August 26). BBC Gardeners' World Magazine. https://www.gardenersworld.com/plants/choosing-a-greenhouse/

How to fertilize blueberry plants. (2016, June 28). Espoma. https://www.espoma.com/fruits-vegetables/how-to-fertilize-blueberry-plants/

How to grow blueberries. (n.d.). Mad about Berries. https://www.madaboutberries.com/blueberries.html

How to grow raspberry bushes. (n.d.). MiracleGro. https://www.miraclegro.com/en-us/library/edible-gardening/how-grow-raspberry-bushes

How to grow seeds in a greenhouse. (2020, April 1). HOLMAN Industries. https://www.holmanindustries.com.au/how-to-grow-seeds-in-a-greenhouse/

How to grow Violas: 5 tips for growing violas. (2020, August 18). GROWING in the GARDEN. https://growinginthegarden.com/how-to-grow-violas-5-tips-for-growing-violas/

How to grow watermelon (Citrullus lanatus). (n.d.). In Seed Savers EXCHANGE. https://www.seedsavers.org/site/pdf/grow-save-watermelons.pdf

How to grow watermelon in containers successfully. (2017, September 18). Gardener KNOW HOW. https://gardenerknowhow.com/grow-watermelon-pot-vertically

How to insulate your greenhouse foundation. (2009, November 4). Doityourself. https://www.doityourself.com/stry/how-to-insulate-your-greenhouse-foundation

How to pollinate plants in a greenhouse. (2020, June 30). Greenhouse Emporium. https://greenhouseemporium.com/blogs/greenhouse-gardening/greenhouse-pollination/

How to store edible flowers. (2020, May 16). Common Farms. https://commonfarms.com/how-to-store-edible-flowers

How to treat Spider Mites. (2019, October 3). GREENERY UNLIMITED. https://greeneryunlimited.co/blogs/plant-care/how-to-treat-spider-mites-on-indoor-houseplants

Iannotti, M. (2019, October 19). *Consider your framing options when building a greenhouse.* The Spruce. https://www.thespruce.com/building-a-greenhouse-choosing-materials-1403234

Iannotti, M. (2021a, July 26). *How to grow and use delicious dill.* the Spruce. https://www.thespruce.com/dill-tips-for-growing-and-using-1402606

Iannotti, M. (2021b, August 31). *How to grow violas in a home garden.* the Spruce. https://www.thespruce.com/growing-violas-1402895

Iannotti, M. (2022, March 11). *How to grow parsley.* the Spruce. https://www.thespruce.com/grow-parsley-1402629

Identify and control Fungus Gnats. (n.d.). GardenTech. https://www.gardentech.com/insects/fungus-gnats

Irrigation Systems. (2015, April 13). Center for Agriculture, Food and the Environment. https://ag.umass.edu/greenhouse-floriculture/greenhouse-best-management-practices-bmp-manual/irrigation-systems

Is cucumber a fruit or a vegetable? (2019, March 22). Healthline. https://www.healthline.com/nutrition/is-cucumber-a-fruit

Isabel. (2020, March 10). *The perfect greenhouse size for your needs*. Greenhouse Hunt. https://www.greenhousehunt.com/greenhouses/perfect-greenhouse-size/

Iseli, M. (2021, September 4). *When to fertilize strawberries? The answer!* PLANTOPHILES. https://plantophiles.com/gardening/when-to-fertilize-strawberries/

Jackson, K. (2019, August 12). *Do it yourself / DIY geodesic greenhouse*. Growing Spaces. https://growingspaces.com/diy-greenhouse/

Johnson, H., & Hickman, G. (n.d.). *Hydroponic vegetable production*. Aggie Horticulture. https://aggie-horticulture.tamu.edu/greenhouse/hydroponics/cucumber.html

Kai. (2008, October 9). *What to do with fresh parsley*. FRUGAL COOKING. https://frugalcooking.com/what-to-do-with-fresh-parsley/

Kevin. (2021, January 29). *Growing dill weed and seeds in the garden*. EPIC GARDENING. https://www.epicgardening.com/growing-dill/

Kuack, D. (2016, August 30). *Monitoring is crucial for growing lettuce and leafy greens year round*. HORT AMERICAS. https://hortamericas.com/blog/news/monitoring-is-crucial-for-growing-lettuce-and-leafy-greens-year-round/

Laliberte, K. (2021, January 24). *Season-extending with row covers and cold frames*. GARDENER'S SUPPLY COMPANY. https://www.gardeners.com/how-to/season-extending-techniques/5063.html

Lamm, Freddie. R. (n.d.). *Advantages and disadvantages of subsurface drip irrigation*. In University of Wisconsin–Madison. https://fyi.extension.wisc.edu/cropirrigation/files/2015/12/Adv-Disadv-SDI-KS-2002-Lamm.pdf

Lampert, E. (2019, March 13). *How to build a simple greenhouse with recycled materials*. Green Building. https://greenbuildingcanada.ca/2019/simple-greenhouse-recycled-materials/

Larano, L. (2020, August 26). *How to care for your basil plant*. OMYSA. https://omysa.com/blogs/planting-101/how-to-care-for-your-basil-plant

Lettuce. (2020, January 29). Wikipedia. https://en.wikipedia.org/wiki/Lettuce

Liburd, O., & Rhodes, E. (2019). *Management of strawberry insect and mite pests in greenhouse and field crops*. In www.intechopen.com. IntechOpen. https://www.intechopen.com/chapters/65144

Lieten, P. (2002, January). *The effect of humidity on the performance of greenhouse grown strawberry*. ResearchGate. https://www.researchgate.net/publication/283370468_The_effect_of_humidity_on_the_performance_of_greenhouse_grown_strawberry

Liles, V. (n.d.). *Homemade greenhouse ideas*. Home Guides. https://homeguides.sfgate.com/homemade-greenhouse-ideas-56300.html

M, A. (2019, November 7). *How to keep a greenhouse from blowing away*. GROW in a Greenhouse. https://www.growinggreenhouse.com/how-to-keep-a-greenhouse-from-blowing-away/

M, A. (2020, January 29). *What is the best soil for greenhouse plants?* GROW in a Greenhouse. https://www.growinggreenhouse.com/what-is-the-best-soil-for-greenhouse-plants/

Macdonald, M. (2021a, April 20). *How to grow California Poppies.* West Coast Seeds. https://www.westcoastseeds.com/blogs/how-to-grow/grow-california-poppy#:~:text=Seeds%20should%20sprout%20in%2014%2D21%20days.&text=Grow%20in%20any%20average%2C%20well

Macdonald, M. (2021b, April 26). *How to grow strawberries.* West Coast Seeds. https://www.westcoastseeds.com/blogs/how-to-grow/grow-strawberries

Machuka, J. (2020, November 16). *Wooden vs metallic greenhouses.* Synnefa. https://synnefa.io/2020/11/16/wooden-vs-metallic-greenhouses/

Managing pests in gardens: Floriculture: Poppy. (n.d.). Statewide Integrated Pest Management Program. http://ipm.ucanr.edu/PMG/GARDEN/FLOWERS/poppy.html

Managing weeds in and around the greenhouse. (2015, March 6). Center for Agriculture, Food, and the Environment. https://ag.umass.edu/greenhouse-floriculture/fact-sheets/managing-weeds-in-around-greenhouse#:~:text=Prior%20to%20mowing%20or%20using

Mann, N. (2022, March 28). *What should I consider when purchasing a used greenhouse?* Wisegeek. https://www.wise-geek.com/what-should-i-consider-when-purchasing-a-used-greenhouse

Markgraf, B. (2018). *How are GMOs made?* SCIENCING. https://sciencing.com/gmos-made-6453138.html

Masabni, J., & King, S. (n.d.). *Dill - How do you grow dill in a garden or in containers?* Texas A&M AgriLife Extension Service. https://agrilifeextension.tamu.edu/library/gardening/dill/

Masabni, J., & Lilliard, P. (n.d.). *How to grow melons.* TEXAS A&M AGRILIFE EXTENSION. https://cdn-ext.agnet.tamu.edu/wp-content/uploads/2014/09/how-to-grow-melons.pdf

Matt. (2020, June 16). *How to dismantle a greenhouse.* South West GREENHOUSES. https://www.swgreenhouses.co.uk/blog/how-to-dismantle-a-greenhouse.

Mcintosh, J. (2021, July 21). *How to grow California Poppies.* the Spruce. https://www.thespruce.com/how-to-grow-and-care-for-california-poppies-4686987#:~:text=As%20long%20as%20temperatures%20remain

Miceli, P. (2009, November 18). *PVC greenhouse frame benefits and drawbacks.* DoItYourself. https://www.doityourself.com/stry/pvc-greenhouse-frame-benefits-and-drawbacks

Michaels, K. (2020, September 15). *5 tips for growing awesome tomatoes in containers.* the Spruce. https://www.thespruce.com/tips-for-growing-tomatoes-in-containers-848216

Miller, A. (2020, September 18). *Growing basil seeds: When to transplant basil seedlings.* KROSTRADE. https://krostrade.com/blog/when-to-transplant-basil-seedlings/

Miller, L. (2020, August 7). *Why pollinate by hand: What is the purpose of hand pollination.* Gardening KNOW HOW. https://www.gardeningknowhow.com/garden-how-to/info/purpose-of-hand-pollination.htm

Mills, L. (2013, January 16). *As the worm turns - The geodesic greenhouse—pros & cons.* Crestone Eagle. https://crestoneeagle.com/as-the-worm-turns-the-geodesic-greenhouse-pros-cons/

Mohammed, N. (2018). *Development of greenhouse lettuce growing techniques in Alberta.* In Alberta Agriculture and Forestry. https://open.alberta.ca/dataset/235fa62d-7339-4e1d-a39a-463baae84249/resource/d50deaf4-fea6-4e05-bdf1-e092a59f1e2b/download/251-15-1.pdf

Monk, J. (2021, April 12). *Types of greenhouse flooring.* Greenhouse Info. https://greenhouseinfo.com/types-greenhouse-flooring/

Morris, W. (2018, November 10). *13 advantages of growing plants within a greenhouse.* Greener Ideal. https://greenerideal.com/guides/13-advantages-of-growing-plants-within-a-greenhouse/

Moulton, M. (2022, March 4). *How much sunlight do marigolds need?* Petal Republic. https://www.petalrepublic.com/marigold-light-requirements/

Mphuthi, P. (2017, August 3). *Tobacco Mosaic virus: Symptoms, transmission, and management.* Farmer's Weekly. https://www.farmersweekly.co.za/crops/field-crops/tobacco-mosaic-virus-symptoms-transmission-management/

Mr. Strawberry. (2020, June 8). *Strawberry plant diseases: Bacteria, fungi, molds & viruses.* STRAWBERRY PLANTS.ORG. https://strawberryplants.org/diseases-fungi-molds/

Murphy, L., & Allen, S. (2021, September 23). *How much does a greenhouse cost?* Forbes ADVISOR. https://www.forbes.com/advisor/home-improvement/greenhouse-cost/

National Gardening Association - Research Division. (n.d.). GARDEN RESEARCH. https://www.gardenresearch.com/index.php?q=show&id=3126

Nazario, B. (2020, September 16). *Health benefits of lettuce.* WebMD. https://www.webmd.com/diet/health-benefits-lettuce

Ojeda–Melchor, L. (2020, April 29). *How to grow violets in containers.* Gardener's Path. https://gardenerspath.com/plants/flowers/grow-violets-containers/

Palynivore. (2019, December 2). Wikipedia. https://en.wikipedia.org/wiki/Palynivore

Parbst, K. (2018, May 27). *Three steps to effective greenhouse humidity control.* GREENHOUSE GROWER. https://www.greenhousegrower.com/technology/three-steps-to-effective-greenhouse-humidity-control/

Pearce, M. (2020, March 19). *How to grow cucumbers in a greenhouse.* ACCESS Garden Products. https://www.garden-products.co.uk/news/growing-under-glass/how-to-grow-cucumbers-in-a-greenhouse/

Pennisi, B. (2003, November 13). *Fertilizer injectors: Selection, maintenance, and calibration.* UGA Cooperative Extension. https://extension.uga.edu/publications/detail.html?number=B1237&title=Fertilizer%20Injectors:%20Selection

Pests and diseases of lettuce crops. (2013, January 1). Queensland Government - Department of Agriculture and Fisheries. https://www.daf.qld.gov.au/business-priorities/agriculture/plants/fruit-vegetable/fruit-vegetable-crops/lettuce/pests-and-diseases-of-lettuce-crops

Photos from a day in the life: California Poppy harvest. (2022, February 2). HERB PHARM. https://www.herb-pharm.com/blogs/farm-stories/photos-from-a-day-in-the-life-california-poppy-harvest#:~:text=Herb%20Pharm%20harvests%20California%20Poppy

Piper, A. (2020, May 18). *How a backyard garden could save you $500 on groceries.* The PENNYHOARDER. https://www.thepennyhoarder.com/save-money/grow-your-own-food/

Plant disease - an overview. (n.d.). ScienceDirect. https://www.sciencedirect.com/topics/medicine-and-dentistry/plant-disease#:~:text=Plant%20disease%20is%20defined%20as

Plant pollination strategies. (n.d.). U.S. Forest Service. https://www.fs.fed.us/wildflowers/pollinators/Plant_Strategies/index.shtml

Planting Poppies in containers: How to care for potted Poppy plants. (2021, October 18). Gardening KNOW HOW. https://www.gardeningknowhow.com/ornamental/flowers/poppy/planting-poppies-in-containers.htm#:~:text=Any%20medium%2Dsized%20container%20is

Planting schedules. (n.d.). Urban Farmer. https://www.ufseeds.com/planting-schedules.html

Poindexter, J. (2019, May 10). *The pros & cons of 18 gardening methods and which one is right for you.* MorningChores. https://morningchores.com/gardening-methods-pros-cons/

Poudel, M., & Dunn, B. (2017, March). *Greenhouse carbon dioxide supplementation.* Oklahoma State University. https://extension.okstate.edu/fact-sheets/greenhouse-carbon-dioxide-supplementation.html

Preparing site for a greenhouse. (n.d.). Thompson & Morgan. https://www.thompson-morgan.com/buying-guides/preparing-site-for-greenhouse

Pritts, M. (n.d.). *In raspberry, for every hour delay in cooling, shelf life can be reduced by one day.* Postharvest - Fruits, Vegetables, and Ornamentals. https://www.postharvest.biz/en/news/in-raspberry-for-every-hour-delay-in-cooling-shelf-life-can-be-reduced-by-one-day/_id:79270/

Private and non–commercial greenhouse definition. (n.d.). Law Insider. https://www.lawinsider.com/dictionary/private-and-noncommercial-greenhouse

Procedure of planting raspberry seeds. (n.d.). Andra Farm. https://m.andrafarm.com/_andra.php?_i=0-tanaman-kelompok&topik=menanam&kelompok=Raspberry&_en=ENGLISH

Putatunda, P. (2016, July 2). *Growing lettuce in containers.* Balcony Garden Web. https://balconygardenweb.com/growing-lettuce-in-containers-how-to-grow-lettuce-in-pots/

Quonset–style greenhouse plans. (n.d.). SIMPLIFIED BUILDING. https://www.simplifiedbuilding.com/projects/greenhouse-frame

Quotes about greenhouses (42 quotes). (n.d.). Quote Master. https://www.quotemaster.org/Greenhouses

Rare plant, the Diamond-Petaled California poppy, flourishing this spring at LLNL facility. (n.d.). Lawrence Livermore National Laboratory. https://www.llnl.gov/news/rare-plant-diamond-petaled-california-poppy-flourishing-spring-llnl-facility

Rasanen, O. (2021, November 12). *How can you maintain the ideal humidity in a greenhouse?* Ruuvi. https://ruuvi.com/how-can-you-maintain-the-ideal-humidity-in-a-greenhouse/

Raspberries. (n.d.). Old Farmer's Almanac. https://www.almanac.com/plant/raspberries#

Raspberry care instructions. (n.d.). Arbor Day Foundation. https://www.arborday.org/trees/fruit/care-raspberry.cfm

Read, M. (2020, November 23). *Is a Walipini sunken greenhouse right for you?* Green Home Gnome. https://www.greenhomegnome.com/walipini-style-sunken-greenhouse/

Reducing humidity in the greenhouse. (2015, March 6). Center for Agriculture, Food and the Environment. https://ag.umass.edu/greenhouse-floriculture/fact-sheets/reducing-humidity-in-greenhouse

Rhoades, H. (2021, June 23). *Light requirements for tomatoes – How much sun do tomato plants need.* Gardening KNOW HOW. https://www.gardeningknowhow.com/edible/vegetables/tomato/how-much-sun-do-tomato-plants-need.htm

Rodriguez, A. (n.d.). *These peel and stick floor tiles will give your kitchen an affordable new look.* SF GATE. https://homeguides.sfgate.com/peel-stick-floor-tiles-13771623.html

Rogers, J. (2016, February 23). *Top 10 reasons for having a greenhouse.* OLT. https://outdoorlivingtoday.com/top-10-reasons-for-owning-a-greenhouse/

Roper, M. (2019). *How often do you water marigolds?* Hunker. https://www.hunker.com/13426483/how-often-do-you-water-marigolds

Sawtooth greenhouse. (n.d.). NatureHydro. https://www.naturehydro.com/sawtooth-greenhouse.html

Schiller, L. (2022, January 8). *Essential tips for building a durable walipini greenhouse.* MOTHER EARTH NEWS. https://www.motherearthnews.com/organic-gardening/essential-tips-for-building-a-durable-walipini-greenhouse-zbcz1706/

Schrock, D. (n.d.). *Building and using hotbeds and cold frames.* Extension.missouri.edu; University of Missouri. https://extension.missouri.edu/publications/g6965

Seaman, G. (2022, February 19). *5 things to consider before you buy a greenhouse. Eartheasy.* https://learn.eartheasy.com/articles/5-things-to-consider-before-you-buy-a-greenhouse/

Seed starting: Selecting the best containers for your seedlings. (n.d.). AlboPepper. http://albopepper.com/seed-starting-trays-containers.php

Seladi–Schulman, J. (2020, January 21). *Does Poppyseed oil have benefits?* Healthline. https://www.healthline.com/health/poppy-seed-oil#:~:text=Poppies%20are%20known%20for%20producing

Selvey, T. (n.d.). *How to identify, control and prevent blight on your tomatoes.* GardenTech. https://www.gardentech.com/blog/pest-id-and-prevention/fight-blight-on-your-tomatoes#:~:text=Blight%20spreads%20by%20fungal%20spores

Sexual vs. asexual propagation. (n.d.). General Horticulture. http://generalhorticulture.tamu.edu/lectsupl/Propaga/propaga.html

Shannon. (2022, February 12). *A beautifully efficient DIY dome greenhouse.* OFF GRID World. https://offgridworld.com/a-beautifully-efficient-diy-dome-greenhouse/

Sharaf, B. (2019). *Advantages and disadvantages of drip irrigation.* Civil Engineering. https://civiltoday.com/water-resource-engineering/irrigation/278-advantages-and-disadvantages-of-drip-irrigation

SIERRA GREENHOUSE. (2021, February 4). *10 Different Types of greenhouses | Structures, and designs.* https://sierragreenhouse.com/types-of-greenhouses/

Simple Tek. (2021, June 21). *Greenhouse roof vents - Sawtooth greenhouses.* YouTube. https://www.youtube.com/watch?v=0BwIevydo4M

Smart modular greenhouses turn urban rooftops into gardens. (2015, January 16). SPRING WISE. https://www.springwise.com/smart-modular-greenhouses-turn-urban-rooftops-gardens/

Soil pH levels for plants. (2017, August 12). Old Farmer's Almanac. https://www.almanac.com/plant-ph

Sorensen, D., & Garland, K. (2019). *Plant propagation - Cooperative extension: Garden & yard.* University of Maine Cooperative Extension. https://extension.umaine.edu/gardening/manual/propagation/plant-propagation/

Sparkle - Strawberry plants. (n.d.). Johnny's Selected Seeds. https://www.johnnyseeds.com/fruits/strawberry/sparkle-strawberry-plants-2500.html?cgid=strawberry#start=1

Sparks, B. D. (2018a, August 7). *Four keys to optimal airflow in the greenhouse.* GREENHOUSE GROWER. https://www.greenhousegrower.com/technology/heating-cooling-ventilation/four-keys-to-optimal-air-flow-in-the-greenhouse/

Spengler, T. (2021, August 11). *Greenhouse tree care: Growing fruit trees in a greenhouse.* Gardening KNOW HOW. https://www.gardeningknowhow.com/special/greenhouses/greenhouse-tree-care-growing.htm

Starr, K. (2021, July 20). *How much sun and shade can berries tolerate? A complete guide.* Backyard Homestead HQ. https://backyardhomesteadhq.com/how-much-sun-and-shade-can-berries-tolerate-a-complete-guide/

Stauffer, B., & Spulher, D. (n.d.). *Manual irrigation.* Sustainable Sanitation and Water Management. https://sswm.info/sswm-solutions-bop-markets/inclusive-innovation-and-service-delivery/labour-intensive-technologies/manual-irrigation

Stewart, J. (2009, July 7). B*uilding with galvanized steel: Pros and cons.* DoItYourself. https://www.doityourself.com/stry/building-with-galvanized-steel--pros-and-cons

Strawberry | Plant and fruit. (2019). In Encyclopedia Britannica. https://www.britannica.com/plant/strawberry

Study: Plastic greenhouses in China pose pros and cons. (n.d.). THE UNIVERSITY of RHODE ISLAND. https://web.uri.edu/celsnews/study-plastic-greenhouses-in-china-pose-pros-and-cons/

Subirrigation. (2019, May 21). Wikipedia. https://en.wikipedia.org/wiki/Subirrigation

Sucking pests. (n.d.). Insects in the City. https://citybugs.tamu.edu/factsheets/landscape/sapfeed/#:~:text=Sap%2Dfeeding%20insects

Sustainable farming. (2019, October 10). SUPERIOR FRESH. https://www.superiorfresh.com/blog-reference/the-new-method-of-sustainable-farming

The average water requirement for strawberry plants for the two experimental set. (n.d.). ResearchGate. https://www.researchgate.net/figure/The-average-water-requirement-for-strawberry-plants-for-the-two-experimental-set_fig3_274736508

The different types of attached greenhouses. (2015, April 24). Garden & Greenhouse. https://www.gardenandgreenhouse.net/the-different-types-of-attached-greenhouses/

The importance of bees: Pollination. (2009, October 2). CANADA AGRICULTURE and FOOD MUSEUM. https://bees.techno-science.ca/english/bees/pollination/default.php

The tomato: A versatile, popular and vulnerable crop. (n.d.). The Agricultural Research Council. https://arc.agric.za/Agricultural%20Sector%20News/The%20tomato%20-%20a%20versatile

Thrips. (n.d.). Old Farmer's Almanac. https://www.almanac.com/pest/thrips

Tiara - Organic (F1) cabbage seed. (n.d.). Johnny's Selected Seeds. https://www.johnnyseeds.com/vegetables/cabbage/tiara-organic-f1-cabbage-seed-3626G.html?cgid=cabbage#start=1

Tip #7: Grow all year round with affordable heating options. (n.d.). ARCADIA GLASSHOUSE. https://arcadiaglasshouse.com/greenhouse-tips/greenhouse-affordable-heating-options/ .

Tip #11: Does my greenhouse need a permit? (n.d.). ARCADIA GLASSHOUSE. https://arcadiaglasshouse.com/greenhouse-tips/tip-11-greenhouse-need-permit/

Tip #12: Sizing your greenhouse for optimum utilization of space. (n.d.). ARCADIA GLASSHOUSE. https://arcadiaglasshouse.com/greenhouse-tips/tip-11-sizing-your-greenhouse-for-optimum-utilization-of-space/

Tips for choosing the right size greenhouse. (2015, February 17). Garden & Greenhouse. https://www.gardenandgreenhouse.net/tips-for-choosing-the-right-size-greenhouse/

Tomato: Uses, side effects, interactions, dosage, and warning. (2019). WebMD. https://www.webmd.com/vitamins/ai/ingredientmono-900/tomato

Totemeier, C. (1981, April 19). *Gardening; Greenhouses: A luxury becomes a hobby.* The New York Times. https://www.nytimes.com/1981/04/19/archives/gardening-greenhouses-a-luxury-becomes-a-hobby.html

Turner, D. (n.d.). *How to fertilize Marigolds.* SFGATE. https://homeguides.sfgate.com/fertilize-marigolds-63324.html

Types of cucumbers: Varieties from around the world. (2019, July 12). LEAFY Place. https://leafyplace.com/types-of-cucumbers/

Types of greenhouse coverings. (2012, January 12). GARDENING CHANNEL. https://www.gardeningchannel.com/types-of-greenhouse-coverings/

Types of greenhouses. (2007, June 12). Department of Primary Industries. https://www.dpi.nsw.gov.au/agriculture/horticulture/greenhouse/structures-and-technology/types

Unagi - (F1) cucumber seed. (n.d.). Johnny's Selected Seeds. https://www.johnnyseeds.com/vegetables/cucumbers/unagi-f1-cucumber-seed-4552.html?cgid=cucumbers#start=1

Vernon, J. (2011, August 9). *Greenhouse ventilation.* HARTLEY BOTANIC. https://hartley-botanic.co.uk/magazine/ventilation-ventilation-ventilation/

Vertical Air Flow (VAF) fan. (2018, September 17). Greenhouse MANAGEMENT. https://www.greenhousemag.com/article/cropking-vostermans-vertical-air-flow-vaf-fan/

Volente, G. (2019, July 29). *Best vegetables to grow in a greenhouse.* GREENHOUSE TODAY. https://www.greenhousetoday.com/best-vegetables-to-grow-in-a-greenhouse/

Volente, G. (2021, April 11). *How many tomatoes can one plant produce?* GREENHOUSE TODAY. https://www.greenhousetoday.com/how-many-tomatoes-can-1-plant-produce/

W, M. (2016, February 2). *Greenhouse stores.* Greenhouse Stores. https://www.greenhousestores.co.uk/blog/Growing-Tomatoes-In-A-Greenhouse/

Waddington, E. (2020, November 6). *7 innovative ways to heat your greenhouse in winter.* RURAL SPROUT. https://www.ruralsprout.com/heat-greenhouse/

Warwick, S. (2021, January 8). *Greenhouse growing calendar: A month-by-month guide for delicious crops.* Gardeningetc. https://www.gardeningetc.com/advice/what-to-grow-in-a-greenhouse

Waskosky, A. (2010). *Plant article Orchids: Characteristics.* NORTH DAKOTA STATE UNIVERSITY. https://www.ndsu.edu/pubweb/chiwonlee/plsc211/student%20papers/article10/Awaskoskyhorticulture/characteristics.html#:~:text=Over%20120%20species%20of%20poppy

Watermelons. (n.d.). Old Farmer's Almanac. https://www.almanac.com/plant/watermelons

Waterworth, K. (2019, July 16). *Best greenhouse plants: Good plants to grow in a greenhouse.* Gardening KNOW HOW. https://www.gardeningknowhow.com/special/greenhouses/plants-for-greenhouses.htm

Waterworth, K. (2021, January 2). *Greenhouse gardening supplies: What are common supplies for a greenhouse.* Gardening Know How. https://www.gardeningknowhow.com/special/greenhouses/greenhouse-gardening-supplies.htm

Watkins, K. (2022a, March 7). *What are the pros and cons of a wooden greenhouse?* HomeQuestionsAnswered. https://www.homequestionsanswered.com/what-are-the-pros-and-cons-of-a-wooden-greenhouse.htm

Watkins, K. (2022b, March 8). *What are the pros and cons of an aluminum greenhouse?* HomeQuestionsAnswered. https://www.homequestionsanswered.com/what-are-the-pros-and-cons-of-an-aluminum-greenhouse.htm

Watson, M. (2019). *The ins and outs of tasty cabbage.* the Spruce Eats. https://www.thespruceeats.com/types-of-cabbages-2215899

Watson, M. (2021, July 19). *Use dill as both a herb and a spice.* the Spruce. https://www.thespruceeats.com/all-about-dill-4117140

Weaver, R. (2021, December 18). *How often to water chives.* Homestead Gardens. https://www.homesteadgardenspa.com/blog/watering-chive-plants/?amp=1

Webb, A. (2022, April 2). *How much sunlight does watermelon need?* Blueberry Farm. https://www.columbusblueberry.com/about-berries/how-much-sunlight-does-watermelon-need.html

What are the advantages and disadvantages of greenhouse kits? (n.d.). Mulberry Greenhouses. https://mulberrygreenhouses.com/blogs/greenhouse-guides/what-are-the-advantages-and-disadvantages-of-greenhouse-kits

What causes pansies to droop? (2020, November 6). SFGATE. https://homeguides.sfgate.com/causes-pansies-droop-60142.html

What is pollination? (2019). U.S Forest Service. https://www.fs.fed.us/wildflowers/pollinators/What_is_Pollination/

What's a better greenhouse frame - galvanized steel or aluminum? (n.d.). Planta GREENHOUSES. https://plantagreenhouses.com/blogs/learn/what-s-a-better-greenhouse-frame-galvanized-steel-or-aluminum

When were greenhouses invented? (n.d.). Greenhouse Hunt. https://www.greenhousehunt.com/faq/when-were-greenhouses-invented/

White, R. A. J. (1982). *Multibay inflated roof polythene greenhouse.* New Zealand Journal of Experimental Agriculture, 10(1), 111–116. https://doi.org/10.1080/03015521.1982.10427852

Whiteflies. (n.d.). Old Farmer's Almanac. https://www.almanac.com/pest/whiteflies

Why bees: The role of bumblebees in greenhouses. (2018, May 8). Double Diamond Farms. https://www.doublediamondacres.com/2018/05/08/why-bees-the-role-of-bumblebees-in-greenhouses/

Why choose an aluminum greenhouse? (n.d.). HARTLEY BOTANIC. https://hartley-botanic.com/guides/why-choose-aluminum-greenhouse-us/

Wiley, D. (2020, June 1). *Grow these delicious berries from your own backyard.* Better Homes and Gardens. https://www.bhg.com/gardening/container/plans-ideas/berries-in-containers/

Will, M. (2020, May 5). *DIY lean-to greenhouse.* Empress of Dirt. https://empressofdirt.net/build-lean-to-greenhouse/

Will, M. (2021, April 20). *How to transplant raspberry bushes.* Empress of Dirt. https://empressofdirt.net/transplant-raspberries/

Worst, R. (2020, November 18). *18 types of marigolds to brighten up your garden.* WorstRoom. https://worstroom.com/types-of-marigolds/

Wotzak, R. (2018, September 11). *Easy-to-Build Cold Frame.* Fine Gardening. https://www.finegardening.com/project-guides/fruits-and-vegetables/easy-build-cold-frame

Made in the USA
Columbia, SC
29 May 2023